NOVELL®
NetWare Lite™
Step by Step

by Dirk Larisch

Abacus

A Data Becker Book

Copyright © 1992	Abacus 5370 52nd Street SE Grand Rapids, MI 49512
Copyright © 1992	Data Becker, GmbH Merowingerstrasse 30 4000 Duesseldorf, Germany
Managing Editor	Jim D'Haem
Editors	Robbin Markley, Al Wier
Technical Editor	Mike Bergsma
Cover Art	John Plummer/Dick Droste

```
Larisch, D. (Dirk). 1958-
    Novel Netware lite step-by-step / Dirk Larisch.
        p.   cm.
    Incluides index.
    ISBN  1-55755-154-5 : $24.95
    1. Operating systems (Computers)  2. NetWare (Computer file)
  I. Title.
QA76.76.063L3655   1991
005.7'1369--dc20
                                                        92-1734
                                                            CIP
```

Printed in U.S.A.

10 9 8 7 6 5 4 3 2 1

Table of Contents

Foreword

The "lite craze" has now reached the software industry. When first working with the new product from Novell, you will probably ask yourself just what is so "lite" about NetWare Lite?

It won't take you long to find out that there is a very big difference between the "large" NetWare versions (2.2 and 3.11) and NetWare Lite. This is not a disadvantage because NetWare Lite "points" in a very different direction. Just think of NetWare Lite as the little brother of NetWare 2.2 or NetWare 3.11.

NetWare Lite is an extension of the DOS operating system, designed especially for network use. With no other system it's possible to create a network from two available DOS computers. The advantage of NetWare Lite is that, except for some additional hardware (network cards, cabling) and NetWare Lite, there are no other requirements to be met.

NetWare Lite is used to create small networks, particularly those in which existing computers are to be retained and further used. NetWare Lite also provides easy access to the large versions of NetWare (2.2, 3.11). Data exchange and access to certain resources are possible in both directions.

Most NetWare Lite users won't be able to find the information they need in the rather sketchy handbook. The individual topics aren't discussed in detail.

For this reason you will find more comprehensive and thorough explanations which will soon make the use of NetWare Lite seem like "child's play" to you. Think of this book as an introduction to working with NetWare Lite, and also as a reference work which will simplify your daily work with NetWare Lite. Also, the problem-oriented approach to the individual topics is used in this book.

In addition to the material specific to NetWare Lite, a separate chapter containing general information on network use is included. There you will find specifics on the various network topologies, and on different cable hook-up options. This material makes up a stand alone chapter which you can read to find out what hardware requirements are needed for the network application. The necessary information is presented with reference to a model network.

My special thanks goes out to Mr. Leonhardt of Novell for his extremely friendly and helpful support in the creation of this book.

I hope in any case that you will have a lot of fun with NetWare Lite and with "NetWare Lite Step by Step"...

Dirk Larisch

Working with this Book

While reading this book, you'll notice the following formats, which indicate the actions that should be performed:

Courier   Text displayed in this font and size represents information that you should enter using the keyboard. It also represents text that will be displayed on the screen.

dir [Enter]

Keys that you should type from the keyboard will appear as key icons in the text. For example, if you see [A], you should press this key. Cursor movement keys are also displayed in this way (e.g., [↑] indicates that you should press the Up arrow key).

[Alt] [E]

This type of entry indicates that you must press and hold the [Alt] key while pressing the [E] key.

[Alt][E] + [Q]

When you see this type of entry you should hold [Alt] while pressing [E], then release both keys and press [Q].

[F1]

A keystroke, such as [F1], refers to one of the function keys. These keys are usually located in a single row above the number keys at the top of your keyboard or in two columns on the left.

:DOS [Enter]

This represents a command that must be entered at the NetWare console. The colon, which should not be entered, is used only to indicate that this is a console mode command. The following symbols identify special sections of text:

☞   This symbol indicates that the section contains useful information about working in the network.

✎   This symbol indicates an important note.

1.   Installation

Before we begin installing NetWare Lite, we will provide some information on the principles and structure of a network.

The next chapter is for those of you who have not worked with networks, but would like to know more. You will learn their purpose and how to use the network. You will learn a few technical terms which will "turn up" during any discussion of network use.

In addition, this chapter includes various characteristics and principles of the different types of networks. Explanations of various network architectures and the composition of a network are also included.

This chapter also discusses the composition of a model network. You will learn what hardware and software requirements are needed to construct a network. For the sake of simplicity, we will begin with a minimal configuration consisting of two computers. Additional information will be discussed in more detail later in this book.

If your familiar with the structure of a network and have already worked with networks, you can simply skip this chapter and begin with the installation of NetWare Lite in Chapter 2. However, if you've never worked with networks, carefully read this chapter.

1.1   The Network Principle

In addition to the use of PCs as single user computers, the use of networks in many workplace environments is increasing. A network is the connection of several individual computers that share data and resources.

Before discussing the components of a network in detail, let's define the term "network".

The simplest type of network is the connection of two computers that (data processing devices) exchange data and access to common hardware components (resources).

The following are three essential characteristics of a network:

1.   Connectivity

      One requirement of a network is the connection of two or more
      computers. In this case one computer assumes the supervisory
      tasks of the system (e.g., the allocation of resources). This
      master computer is called the *file server* or *server*.
      Additional information will be discussed in more detail
      later in this book.

2.   Common Data Access

      Cmmon data access is another characteristic of a network. It
      is possible, for example, for any of the various workstations
      to access the same file.

3.   Resource Management

      The third feature of a network environment is the common
      use of *resources*. Resources, according to Webster, are
      available means, supplies or assets. In the data processing
      world the term relates to the peripheral devices used. These
      include printers, hard disks, modems, scanners, etc.

      These peripheral devices are ordinarily attached to the
      server to make them available at a central location. An
      advantage of a network is that it's possible for you to gain
      access to these devices from any of the workstations.

You can access the hard disk of the server (the common data
access) and send a print job to a printer connected to another
computer within the network. Supervision is handled by the
system of the individual network.

Besides these three basic features of a network, there are other
features that can be used with a network. It is quite clear from
these three, which you will soon learn, that it isn't really so
difficult after all.

From the second point in the previous list it's obvious that an
application program intended for use on a network must meet
special requirements. What happens, for example, when two users
want to make changes to the same data in a file simultaneously?
Which user will access the data first? Will both changes be
accepted?

Let's suppose that you are manipulating a given database by
changing individual data entries. At the same time, another

network user would like to access this very same database. This can be done as long as the second user is only reading the data. As soon as the user tries to change something in this database, problems occur.

If a second user wants to make a change in a data entry which you're currently processing, how does the application program know which change to accept? Both changes cannot be made simultaneously. Obviously this would lead to a data collision.

This is where the network supervision of the application program begins. Each program utilized within a network must contain available mechanisms so that such a collision of data can be prevented. In the case of most programs, this supervision ensures that any data entry currently in process can never be changed by another user. Other users have a "read" access to the item in question. Any write access is prevented.

Besides the possibility of locking individual data entries (record locking), you can provide a complete database with a lock (file locking). This locking of files, or entries, is usually accomplished by using special mechanisms which control network access and help prevent any problems before they occur. The mechanisms used by various network programs are very similar in principle, but their execution is often very different.

The most recently developed programs for network use are now using *field locks*. Individual fields, instead of complete records, can be blocked from write access by other users.

DOS also makes the SHARE command available for NetWare Lite users. This is loaded on each individual workstation to provide basic file and record locking support for the workstation only. This is necessary for multitasking environments, such as Microsoft Windows, where more than one program can access the same file on a single workstation.

Even programs that don't meet the requirements for network use can be used on a network. In this case you must ensure that data collisions are prevented, for example, by restricting the use of this program to a single user.

1.2   Why Use a Network

Perhaps you will want to ask why you need a network. When is a network sensible and justified? Is it possible to use several single-user computers? These and similar questions will now be discussed in more detail.

The answers to the previous questions require that you know which tasks can be performed on a network. Basically, the tasks and the steps necessary aren't different from those on a single-user computer. It doesn't matter whether a single-user computer is used or whether the workstation is linked to a network. Nevertheless, the network workstation represents something special. This becomes obvious as soon as the user attempts to load a text file, which is currently being used by another network user. In this case a message appears indicating that this particular file is temporarily unavailable.

Besides this basic difference between a single-user computer and a network workstation, we've mentioned another difference earlier. This difference is obvious, for example, whenever a database is being processed with an application program that's activated by several users. Whenever one user makes a change in a data entry, which is then accessed immediately by a second user, the latter will have immediate access to the updated entry.

As you can see from these examples, the use of a network has both advantages and disadvantages. For example, you have the current data immediately available on a network, but you must "pay for" these updates by relinquishing access to certain data. However, on a network it's possible, for example, to gain access to the same printer from several local workstations. This printer is called a *network printer*. Certain network setups allow access to this printer from different workstations. By doing this you can save yourself the cost of buying a separate printer for each individual workstation.

The more common resources used, the greater the cost advantage of a network. For example, if ten workstations have access to a single (expensive) laser printer, the cost of linking the ten workstations is "outweighed" by the cost of the ten laser printers. The advantages are:

- Utilization of common resources, such as printers, hard disks, etc.
- Access to a common store of data and constant updating.
- Possibilities for data exchange.
- Savings in the cost of hardware, depending on the size of the network.

As you can see, there are some advantages of using the network. In the next chapter, the individual components needed for a network will be discussed.

1.3 Data Security

As soon as you work with networks, you will need to know about data security, which we will discuss in more detail. "Security" is both the loss of data due to unforeseen system malfunctions within the network (hard disk crash), and also (undesired) access to data by unauthorized persons.

1.3.1 Protecting data from unauthorized access

The utilization of a network always imposes special demands on data security. Is it possible to prevent one user from gaining access to certain data on the network?

In the case of the network systems currently on the market, the answer to this question is yes. This can be done via the use of special access rights which make it possible to grant to a user only those rights he or she actually needs. You are also able to grant certain access rights under NetWare Lite, without which it is not possible to gain access to any file on the hard disk of a server or a network printer.

Further protection against data misuse is the use of a *user recognition scheme*. Each user wanting to work in a NetWare Lite network must first announce his or her presence. This procedure, called "logging in", requires that the user enter the assigned username (user-ID) and a password. This entry is then checked by the system and only if the data is correct will the user be allowed to work on the network. If the user should enter the wrong password, for example, access will be denied to the system.

If these security mechanisms are applied under NetWare Lite and used correctly, it will be very difficult for an unauthorized individual to gain access to the network.

But always keep in mind that the data stored on a NetWare Lite server is stored on the local hard disk of a "normal" computer. To make the protection perfect, you must also restrict access to the computer itself.

1.3.2 Backing up data

Besides the protection of data in a network from unauthorized access, backing up your data is also an important part of data security.

The most secure, but time consuming type of data security is backing up, at regular intervals, all data in the network. Such a data security policy normally involves the daily backup of data on a tape drive (streamer) or on floppy disks.

The security system you will use and the frequency of data backup are something you must decide for yourself or discuss with your systems manager (network manager).

1.4　The Components of a Network

Now that you have received information about networks in the previous section, the general components of a network will now be discussed.

As previously mentioned, the term network (in general) refers to the interconnection of several pieces of hardware. The connection of individual computers into a network is created, in hardware terms, by using certain network components. Among these are the necessary network cards (adapters) for the individual computers and the cabling between the separate network components, which must be suitable transfer media (cables). In order to identify the individual components that comprise the network, these components are assigned specific addresses, called *nodes*.

The node addresses are usually entered on the network card, and are unique throughout the world. Each producer of such cards is assigned a certain group of numbers that can be used.

The structure of a network also includes, in addition to the network cards utilized and the associated linkage, the form of general access to the network. Among these address methods are currently two which are very widely used: CSMA/CD and token passing. Besides the different access methods, the network architecture (or network topology) used is also important in a network. Network architecture appears in various forms: star, bus or ring.

Assembled from all these components is a network system, there are currently three types of networks which are most often used: Ethernet, ARCnet and token ring. The last named is a special form from IBM. The network type depends on many factors, which are the topology, the network card used and the access method.

In addition to the hardware components, a network also requires software, which controls the system. The programs that make up this software form a *network operating system*.

A computer in a network is called a *workstation*. The person working at such a workstation is called the *user*. Those components of a network that are available to all users, for example, printers, hard disks, etc., are called *resources*.

Normally, a specially configured computer controls the entire network system. This master computer is also called the *server* or *file server*.

A special type of file server is represented by the *print server*. A print server can be set up to control all of the printing on the network. This decreases the file server's work and can increase the performance of the entire network.

If the device units combined into a network are all located within a single building, the network is called a *LAN (Local Area Network)*.

Unlike the LAN, *Wide Area Network (WAN)* indicates a network where the individual units are installed in different buildings, or in different cities or countries.

To simplify our discussion of a network system, the most important components of the network system will be described individually at this point, as well as their significance to the network as a whole. We will discuss the master computers (file servers, print servers), the work stations and the software necessary for network implementation.

1.4.1 The server

A file server or server is the "brains" of each and every network; it's responsible for all the supervisory tasks within the network. Among these are the management of the individual network resources, as well as the allocation of certain network services.

For example, the server controls all access to the data on the network. It must determine which users can access a given file and what changes can be made.

When network printers are used, the management of print jobs from different workstations takes place using *queues*. When a print job is sent to a network printer, it is sequentially placed in a print queue where the jobs wait to be processed by the printer. These must also be managed and supervised. With NetWare Lite, this also falls within the task range of the file server.

The file server makes data exchange (data communication) possible within a network. It can also establish links with other networks to gain access to data and resources normally unavailable.

The tasks of a file server are as follows:

- Managing network resources.
- Supervising and controlling print jobs.
- Managing access rights and the allocation of programs and data.
- Providing communication services.

The tasks performed on a file server must be activated or supervised by a specific person. In a network, this person is the *network manager* or *supervisor*.

The network manager is responsible for the supervision and control of the network, and has all access rights to the system. Only a user with the privileges of a supervisor can assign new user-IDs.

Under NetWare Lite any computer in the network can be declared a server. This feature of NetWare Lite allows you to access the resources of any computer in the network. You are then able to include several file servers in a single network (up to 25).

1.4.2   The print server

Although this particular type of server does not exist under NetWare Lite, the print server will nevertheless be explained at this time.

This special form of file server is responsible for part of the work originally assigned to the file server, specifically the management of all print jobs. It's not absolutely necessary, as in the case of file servers, that a print server be used in a network. The file server usually handles this task itself.

As previously mentioned, a stand-alone print server of this type is not used under NetWare Lite. There the file server controls the network printers and the printing of tasks.

1.4.3   The workstation (client)

This component of a network has already been mentioned. Essentially every computer linked to the network, on which it is possible for a user to work, is called a *workstation* or *client*.

A workstation is a computer from which a user can gain access to the resources of a network. For example, at a workstation, you can load an application program from the hard disk of any server and also obtain access to the data stored there. From a workstation it is also possible to access a printer attached to a server in order to take care of any printing desired. So think of a workstation (client) as a "normal" single user computer that is also linked to a network.

Under NetWare Lite it's also possible to use a computer as both a server and a client (workstation). For this you only need to enter the appropriate option (server/client) during installation. The server will then assume responsibility for managing its resources. However, you'll also be able to use it as a normal workstation.

A server, which can also be used as a workstation, is called a *non-dedicated server*. The *dedicated file server* is a file server utilized exclusively for the management of the network.

Under NetWare Lite a server will always operate in the non-dedicated mode. In addition to management tasks, you are also able to use any server as a workstation.

1.4.4   The network operating system

Another very important component of a network is the *network operating system*. With this the network is "driven"; without the use of such an operating system the utilization of a network is not possible. For the sake of simplicity, compare this with the utilization of the DOS operating system on a single user computer. You wouldn't be able to use such a computer without the DOS operating system.

There are various network operating systems because each network supplier makes its own operating system available. In this book, you 'll find information on the NetWare Lite operating system.

NetWare Lite makes it possible to set up a network inexpensively. You don't need to dedicate a computer as a file server, as required for NetWare Version 3.11.

Another difference, with regard to NetWare 2.2 and 3.11, is that you don't need to set up the individual hard disks in any special way under NetWare Lite. You can install NetWare Lite on any "normal" PC within minutes, without having to make any software changes on the computer. The current version of Netware Lite supports the following operating systems: MS-DOS 3.x, 4.x, 5.x and DR DOS 6.0.

With NetWare Lite you can connect the hardware of two computers and install the NetWare Lite program. The only hardware requirement to be met is the use of network cards and the appropriate cabling.

Please note that it is absolutely necessary that you have one copy of NetWare Lite per workstation (client). If you install a single copy of NetWare Lite within a network, problems can occur.

In a NetWare Lite network it is possible for any of the computers to be declared the server and make its resources available. Then any computer that was declared a workstation (client) can access such a computer.

It is also possible to add several servers into a network; each computer can be utilized as a server and/or client. If a computer is to be utilized as a workstation (client) and must make its resources available (server), this computer must be declared a client/server. The problems that can result from the client/server principle will be discussed in Chapter 2 of this book.

This type of network, called a *"peer-to-peer network"*, doesn't require a dedicated file server. Any computer on the network can act as both a workstation and a file server.

1.5   Network Architecture

Network architecture or network topology refers to the arrangement of the individual computers within a network; arrangement meaning the hardware connecting the individual computers.

Currently, there are three basic forms:

1.5.1   Ring

The arrangement of the network computers into a ring system can be best seen with reference to the following figure:

In this type of network, each computer is linked to the following one by a cable. By doing this, a ring is formed. In this way, the last computer closes the ring and the network is complete. Each workstation has a fixed predecessor and a fixed successor. Each workstation functions like a transfer computer; the transfer of data from one computer to another always requires that the data be relayed by the computers lying between the two.

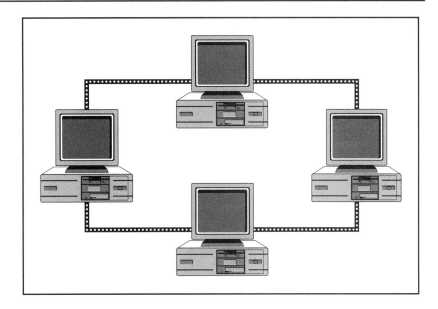

Network Ring

The data is always retransmitted each time it is relayed by a workstation. The result is similar to a signal amplifier, resulting in very high signal reliability.

Another advantage of the ring system is that the transmission range of such a system is so vast because of the amplification of the transmitted signal; almost no losses occur.

The expansion of a ring network can also be carried out at very little expense, because it is always possible to place a new unit between existing workstations.

The ring configuration also has a disadvantage. A break at any point in the ring "disables" the entire system. Such an interruption can occur, for example, when one workstation is down, or from a defective cable.

A well known example of this topology is the IBM Token Ring network.

1.5.2   Bus

The bus system will now be described, by first referring to the following diagram:

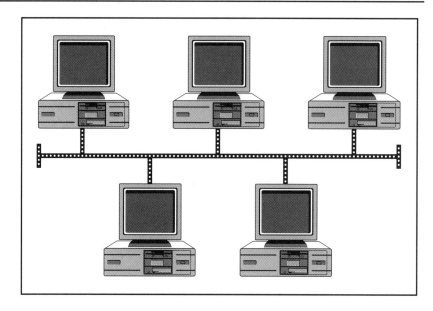

Network Bus

The term *bus* is a line (bus) which is accessed by the individual workstations.

With the network bus, a cable (segment) is used to connect the individual workstations to each other and the file server. The bus must terminate at both ends with a terminal resistor or terminator.

Similar to a ring, a bus can also be expanded at any time by connecting additional workstations. But, under certain circumstances, you can reach the limits of expansion; there is a limit to the length of the cables.

The most common type of bus network in use today is the *Ethernet network*.

One special type of bus topology is the *tree topology*. This also appears as a bus; but there is a further subdivision of the individual branches, resulting in a hierarchical structure.

1.5.3   Star

A star network is illustrated with the following drawing.

The individual workstations of this topology are arranged around the file server in the shape of a star.

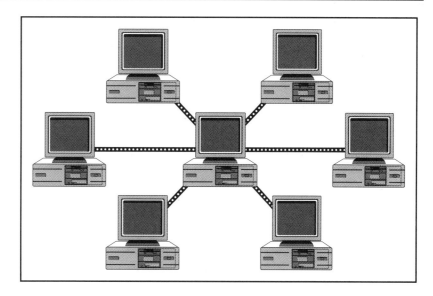

Network Star

However, there are disadvantages to this type of network. You will need a lot of cable to construct such a system; each workstation must be connected directly to the server. Furthermore, this architecture produces a significant delay in the transmission of data between the individual workstations.

The star topology plays a rather minor role in today's networks.

1.5.4 Mixing architectures

Under some circumstances, the simultaneous use of the three forms is appropriate. You can obtain what is called a *composite form*.

In this way the star topology becomes interesting; it is then possible to "mix" together the bus and the star to make an appropriate architecture available.

1.6 Access Methods

The access methods previously mentioned will be discussed at this time. Without an appropriate access method it is impossible for the individual workstations of a network to access the cable (transmission medium).

The access method determines the steps to be taken by a workstation when accessing the server. The following discussion is restricted to the procedures most frequently used: CSMA/CD and token passing.

1.6.1   CSMA/CD

In the case of the *CSMA/CD (Carrier Sense Multiple Access with Collision Detection)* method, the transmitting workstation first checks whether or not the transmission medium (cable) is free (i.e., whether or not other data is in the process of transmission).

Once the cable is free, the workstation sends its data. If another workstation starts "sending data over the cable" simultaneously, the result is an unavoidable data collision. How should station B know that station A has just transmitted data?

At this point, the principle of collision detection is needed. The CSMA/CD access method recognizes this collision and causes the data to be re-sent by the individual workstations (time-delayed); the user is unaware of this process. CSMA/CD uses an algorithm according to which the data is retransmitted. For example, a priority is established, which is dependent upon the node address of the individual workstation. It was previously mentioned that this node address is stored on the network card (adapter) of the workstation in question.

This is why the node addresses must be unique. The presence of two network boards with the same address in a network causes problems with data transmission.

After the data has been sent by the workstation with the higher priority, the data is retransmitted by the other workstation and both reach the recipient.

The CSMA/CD access method is utilized in an Ethernet network.

1.6.2   Token passing

The operation of the token passing method is entirely different. In this case a token is passed through the network. A token is a specific data structure (bit pattern) which "circulates" from workstation to workstation, allowing the workstation that "owns it" to transmit data.

Whenever a workstation wants to transmit data, it must first access the token to query the access information stored there. If the token is free, the workstation is able to transfer its data through the network. Once the token grants the transmission authorization to the workstation in question, the latter can transfer its data to the token. The token then carries the data to the recipient.

During the time that a particular workstation is transmitting data, no other workstation will be able to transmit data. For that, the token must first grant another transmission authorization. The best known networks for using this method of access are Token Ring, ARCnet and the high speed network FDDI.

1.7   Transmission Media

In addition to deciding on a network topology, you must also decide which form of transmission medium or cable will be used. The most common types of cable will be described in this section.

1.7.1   Coaxial cable

This type of cable consists of an interior conductor and jacket for shielding (copper braid, alufoil). This shielding protects the cable from external disturbances. Coaxial cables allow a relatively high transmission rate (up to 10 MBits/s), so you must use caution when laying the cable; avoid any appliances which may cause disturbance. Linkage, using coaxial cables, is generally used in an Ethernet or ARCnet network, in which case the cable ends must be equipped with terminal resistors or network terminators.

There are essentially three types of Ethernet cabling: Thin Ethernet, Thick Ethernet and Cheapernet.

Quite frequently, the terms Thin Ethernet and Cheapernet are used interchangably. However, this is not correct; the Thin Ethernet is distinguished, unlike the Cheapernet cabling, by better shielding, which increases the maximum cable length. The Thin Ethernet cable can be recognized by the colored shielding (for example, gray), while the Cheapernet cable (RG58) is always black.

In addition to the Thin Ethernet, there is also a cable with the name Thick Ethernet. This cable is also called yellow cable, because of its yellow jacketing.

Because the Thick Ethernet cable has better shielding, it is used where the maximum extension length of the Thin Ethernet cabling is not sufficient (max. 900 feet per cable segment; with Cheapernet only 600 feet). With Thick Ethernet you can stretch this to 1600 feet per cable segment.

1.7.2   Twisted pair conductors

A *twisted pair* is any cable with two interior wires which spiral with respect to one another. While this type of cable is very cheap, it has the disadvantage that the shielding against disturbance is very slight. A simple example of this cable is ordinary telephone line, in which several wires are twisted together. Normally this type of cable is called *unshielded twisted pair (UTP)*; there is also a shielded form of this cable type, called *shielded twisted pair (STP)*. In an STP cable the individual wires are shielded with respect to one another, making them less susceptible to disturbances.

The IBM Token Ring network uses this type of cable.

1.7.3   Fiber optics conductors

Fiber Optics cable is the most expensive type of network cable. With this type of cable, data is transmitted in the form of light waves. Fiber optics cable has an interior conductor made of glass or plastic, which is enclosed by a jacket for protection.

Shielding against electrical or magnetic interference isn't necessary because it has no effect upon the glass fiber cable. The greatest advantage of a glass fiber cable is the high transmission rates and the flexibility in the maximum size of the network. Of course, these advantages entail very high acquisition costs.

1.8   The Standard Network

Reference was already made on several occasions to various networks which may currently be considered standard. The most important features of these networks will be discussed in more detail later in this book.

1.8.1   Ethernet networks

Ethernet is a network that's built on the bus topology and utilizes the CSMA/CD access procedure. In an Ethernet network, transmission rates of up to 10MBits/s are common, with the most recent versions allowing transmission rates of up to 20MBits/s. The transmission medium ordinarily used is Thick Ethernet cable.

The maximum length of a cable segment is 500 meters with Thick Ethernet cable. The attachment of a workstation to the bus is accomplished by using a transceiver and a suitable cable (drop cable) which is strung from the bus to the workstation (max. 50 meters).

Expansion of an Ethernet network, beyond the maximum suggested cable length, requires the use of repeaters. A combination of Thin and Thick Ethernet cabling is also possible within the network.

1.8.2   ARCnet networks

Unlike Ethernet, the access procedure used in an ARCnet network is token passing. The topologies possible under ARCnet include the bus and the tree.

When compared with those of an Ethernet network, the transmission rates under ARCnet are very modest. Currently, transmission rates can reach a maximum of 5 MBits/s. However, rates of up to 100 MBits/s have been reached experimentally, by using glass fiber cable as the transmission medium.

ARCnet cabling uses *hubs* (distributors); there are both active and passive hubs. The individual workstations are connected to these hubs. A maximum of 4 connections to a passive hub is possible (in the case of an active hub, up to 16 connections are possible).

1.8.3   IBM Token Rings

The Token Ring network type is a special development by IBM, which uses token passing as the access procedure.

Although the topology used (from a physical point of view) is essentially a bus, a (logical) ring, however, results because of the transmission protocol used.

The transmission speeds move within a range from 4 MBits/s up to 16 MBits/s or 100 MBits/s (fiber optics), in the case of the most recent developments.

The cabling used is the twisted pair, either shielded (STP) or unshielded (UTP) cables are used.

The distribution of the individual connections within a token ring is accomplished by a distributor, also called a *wire center* by IBM.

1.8.4   Looking ahead to future developments

In addition to the standard network types described, there are other network types which will eventually be used. For example, there is a network called *FDDI (Fiber Distributed Data Interface)*. This is a "descendant" of the Token Ring in which transmission rates of up to 100 MBits/s are achieved with the use of light wave conductors. Also, a high-speed network is the *MAN (Metropolitan Area Network)*. This network allows transmission rates of up to 155 MBits/s using fiber optics.

1.9   A Model Network

At this time, we will use the material previously explained to construct a small model network. We will explain which components are necessary for a network and how these individual elements should be assembled to create a network.

Simply connect two computers into an Ethernet network using NetWare Lite. The only requirement is that the two computers already exist and have, until now, been used as single user machines running under DOS.

The following hardware will be required to link two computers together:

- 2-Ethernet network cards. Type NE1000 (for XT computers) or NE2000 (for AT's) from Novell/Eagle, for example.

  The cost of two cards: about $400.00.

  Coaxial cable (Thin Ethernet or Cheapernet) for linking the computers, in which case the appropriate BNC connector should be used.

  The cost of 20 feet of cable with BNC connector plugs at each end: about $15.00.

- 2-BNC T-connectors for attaching the two network cards to the cable; usually included with the network cards.

  2-50 ohm BNC terminators for termination of the cable ends. Grounded BNC terminators, with a grounding wire attached, are also available. You must use one grounded BNC terminator and one standard BNC terminator to properly install the network.

  The price for 2 terminators: about $10.00.

  2-copies of NetWare Lite for the software installation of the network. A separate copy of NetWare Lite is needed for each computer.

  The cost of two copies: about $200.00.

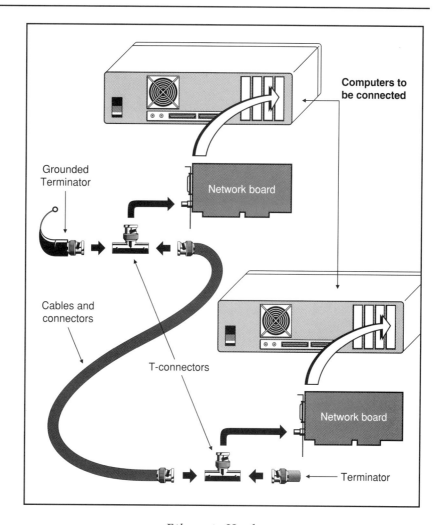

Ethernet   Hardware

The prices listed can vary widely. Comparison shopping is a good idea with regard to all the listed items. Please keep in mind that most of these components are also available by mail order; you may also want to check the prices listed in computer or networking magazines.

Some computer dealers also makes starter kits available. These kits generally contain all items needed for the installation (i.e., both NetWare Lite and the hardware components).

Once you've collected all the components needed, you will then have to install the network cards (adapters) in the two computers. For this, open up the computer and insert the adapter card in one of the available slots. The manual that accompanies the network card will provide additional information regarding the installation of the card and any settings necessary.

Once the network cards are installed in both computers, you can begin laying the cable (Thin Ethernet). First, install a T-connector on each network card, and then link the two computers via the cable by attaching one end of the cable to each of the T-connectors.

Attachment to the BNC connector is achieved by pushing on the plug and then twisting it in a clockwise direction. To remove it, twist it in a counter clockwise direction. As the last step in the hardware phase of the installation, you will now have to mount the terminators on the free ends of the T-connectors, turning them until they are tight (clockwise). With that you have linked the two computers to form a network and have fulfilled the hardware requirements for the use of NetWare Lite.

The following chapter will explain the software installation of NetWare Lite, step by step.

2.   The Installation Of NetWare Lite 1.1

Now that you are familiar with networks, this chapter will
provide information about the installation of the NetWare Lite
software.

If NetWare Lite is already installed on your machine, you can
proceed immediately to the next chapter, where you will find
some important information on using the NetWare Lite network.

In the discussion which follows it is assumed that the hardware
oriented phase of the installation (insertion of the network cards,
etc.) is already complete. The following material deals
exclusively with the installation of the NetWare Lite software.

If you have any problems with the installation of the network
hardware, you can use the model installation found in Chapter 1 of
this book as a guide.

2.1   Before Installation

Before you begin with the installation of NetWare Lite, there are
a few things that should be done. You should take the following
information "to heart"; it will make the work easier for you.

2.1.1   Making backup copies

It is very important, before beginning the installation, that you
make a backup copy of each of the floppy disks supplied in the
NetWare Lite package. If you have NetWare Lite in the 3 1/2"
format, there is only a single disk; otherwise (5 1/4" format) you
will have to copy two floppy disks. To copy individual disks, you
should use the DOS DISKCOPY command as follows:

```
DISKCOPY A: A: Enter
```

For drive B: type:

```
DISKCOPY B: B: Enter
```

2.1.2   Displaying additional information

Once you have made the necessary backup copies, your next step is to display the contents of a special file. This file, entitled README.TXT, is found on the NetWare Lite diskettes and contains important information which was not included in the manual. You will find, in addition to the latest data on NetWare Lite, information on possible problems which may occur when the system is being installed. For this reason, you should display the contents of this file before starting the actual installation. This can be done with the DOS TYPE command.

For example, insert the floppy disk in the A drive and then enter the following at the DOS prompt:

```
TYPE A:\README.TXT  Enter
```

The contents of the file will then appear on the screen. You may also print this file with the following command:

```
TYPE A:\README.TXT > PRN  Enter
```

Once you have read the contents of this file, you should begin with the actual installation of NetWare Lite.

2.1.3   Planning the network

The installation requires some thought, if it is to be kept as brief as possible. Prior to calling the installation program, there are some decisions to be made; this will make the questions easier to answer during installation.

These decisions include, for example, whether the computer on which you are installing NetWare Lite is to function as a client, server or client/server.

Server and Client

A server (file server) is a supervisory computer. This computer controls all supervisory and control functions within a network. The server is also responsible for the communication between the individual users.

The server controls the supervisory tasks and is also the computer that makes its resources available to the attached workstations (clients). These include attached printers and hard disks. A server configured computer decides who may use which programs and which data. It shares its resources with other network participants. If you would like to use the programs stored on other computers within the network, the computer containing these programs must be declared a server (or client server) and your own computer as the client (or client/server).

This is also the case when you want to send something to a network printer. The computer connected to the printer must be defined as a server (or client/server) and the computer sending the print job as the client (or client/server).

A computer designated exclusively as a server is essentially unable to access the resources of other network members; it has no client function.

It's also possible for several servers to be used simultaneously (i.e., more than one computer within the network can be defined as a server).

Unlike the server, a computer configured as a client can access the resources of attached servers. However, this computer cannot make its own resources available to the other network users. This can only be done by a server.

Under NetWare Lite it's possible to declare a computer either as a client or server. In addition, you can also assign a single computer both characteristics. Such a computer, called a client/server, is then able to access the resources of other computers (client mode) and make its own resources available (server mode).

    If you would like to access other computers (servers) and their resources, you will have to implement a client installation. If other network users will have to access your resources (for example, hard disks or other peripheral devices), then you will have to declare your computer a server. NetWare Lite also offers you the option of declaring a computer as both client and server.

The terms client and workstation will be used interchangeably throughout the remainder of the book.

Another very important point required for installation is the identification of the network card utilized. Each computer, on which NetWare Lite is to be installed, requires a special card that's capable of communicating with other computers.

2.1.4   Preparing worksheets

We have only one more recommendation before beginning the installation of NetWare lite; you should prepare a worksheet for each computer that will be on the network.

On the worksheet you should note how NetWare Lite was installed. For example, was the computer installed as a client, a server or a client/server? Which network card was used in this particular machine? What is the capacity of the hard disk used? Which operating system is used on the workstation? This can be an invaluable source of information if problems occur or changes must be made in the future.

2.2   Performing the Installation

Once all necessary preparations and entries have been completed, you are ready to proceed with the installation. The installation of Netware Lite can be a rather complex procedure. The following example should make it relatively simple for you. The installation is comparable to that of a "normal" application program.

The determining factor is a convenient installation program which will help you through the individual phases of the installation. The number of data entries necessary for NetWare Lite has also been reduced to a minimum.

If you already have experience with other Novell products (NetWare 2.2, 3.11, etc.), you will undoubtedly "breeze through" the installation of NetWare Lite. In comparison with that of the other NetWare products, the installation of NetWare Lite is practically "child's play". You will see, NetWare Lite is installed "in a flash".

The following discussion assumes that the installation is being carried out from a 3 1/2" floppy diskette. If you have NetWare Lite on 5 1/4" diskettes, the procedure is almost identical. You are only asked to insert the second disk, containing the network driver, at a certain point in the installation procedure. Below we will list the individual steps necessary for installation. Please remember that the hardware step of the installation should have already been completed.

1.   Start the computer on which NetWare Lite is to be installed. As previously mentioned, the computer can use any MS DOS version above 3.2 or DR DOS 6.0 or higher.

      There is no need to make any changes to the computer. Also, the installation will not affect any of the data or applications currently on the computer. A directory is set up, into which the individual Netware Lite files are copied.

2.   Insert the NetWare Lite disk in drive A: (or B:) and log to drive A: with:

A: [Enter]

3.   Start the INSTALL program with:

INSTALL [Enter]

Soon the Main Menu of the installation program will appear on the screen, as shown in the following illustration:

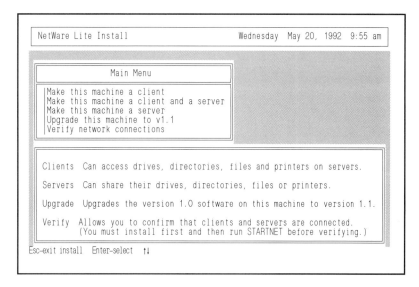

```
┌──────────────────────────────────────────────────────────────────────┐
│ NetWare Lite Install                    Wednesday  May 20, 1992  9:55 am│
│ ┌─────────────────────────────────────────────┐                       │
│ │                   Main Menu                   │                       │
│ │ Make this machine a client                    │                       │
│ │ Make this machine a client and a server       │                       │
│ │ Make this machine a server                    │                       │
│ │ Upgrade this machine to v1.1                  │                       │
│ │ Verify network connections                    │                       │
│ └─────────────────────────────────────────────┘                       │
│ ┌──────────────────────────────────────────────────────────────────┐  │
│ │ Clients  Can access drives, directories, files and printers on servers.│
│ │                                                                    │  │
│ │ Servers  Can share their drives, directories, files or printers.   │  │
│ │                                                                    │  │
│ │ Upgrade  Upgrades the version 1.0 software on this machine to version 1.1.│
│ │                                                                    │  │
│ │ Verify   Allows you to confirm that clients and servers are connected.│
│ │          (You must install first and then run STARTNET before verifying.)│
│ └──────────────────────────────────────────────────────────────────┘  │
│ Esc-exit install  Enter-select  ↑↓                                     │
└──────────────────────────────────────────────────────────────────────┘
```

The Main Menu of the installation program

Before continuing the remaining steps of the installation, the individual items in the Main Menu will be explained.

The individual entries in the Main Menu have the following purpose:

Make this machine a client

The computer will be configured as a workstation or client. Access to other computers, which were declared servers, will be made possible. The resources of this computer, however, cannot be made available to any other network user.

Make this machine a client and a server

The computer in question will be setup as both a client and a server. Access to other servers will be possible (client mode); this computer can also make its own resources available to other network users (server mode).

Make this machine a server

The selection of this menu item will configure the computer as a
server. The resources of this computer are available to other
network users.

Upgrade this machine to v1.1

If NetWare Lite Version 1.0 is installed on the computer, this
menu option will upgrade the NetWare Lite software to Version
1.1.

Verify network connections

This menu item allows you to check the hardware connections
within a network. If you experience problems with the network,
this will help determine if its a hardware (cabling) problem or a
problem with the software. Please note, however, that this menu
item cannot be used before completing the installation; it requires
the activation of the network driver. This means, for example,
that before testing the cabling you must first start the installation,
activate the network and, call the INSTALL program to activate
this menu item (more on this later).

4.   Use the cursor keys to select the desired option and press
     Enter.

     If the mode of one of the computers (client to server or
     vice versa) needs to be changed in the future, simply
     rerun the INSTALL program and select the new option
     from the menu.

5.   If you have selected the installation of the client mode, you
     will be asked to enter the drive and directory containing
     NetWare Lite. The default shown is C:\NWLITE. You
     should enter the desired path and press Enter, or simply
     press Enter to accept the default.

     This entry disappears if server or client/server mode is
     selected. In that case, NetWare Lite will be installed
     automatically on drive C: (the boot drive), in a directory
     named \NWLITE.

     If NetWare Lite was already installed on the
     computer, and you run the installation program again,
     you will be asked whether or not the existing

installation is to be overwritten. Choose YES to reinstall, or NO to exit the INSTALL program.

   It's possible to run NetWare Lite in the client mode on a workstation without a hard disk (floppy disk installation). This is described in Section 2.5.

6.   If you install NetWare Lite in server or client/server mode, you will be asked to enter the name of the server. You should give the server a meaningful name; it's important if the network consists of more than one server. The following illustration shows the appropriate entry field.

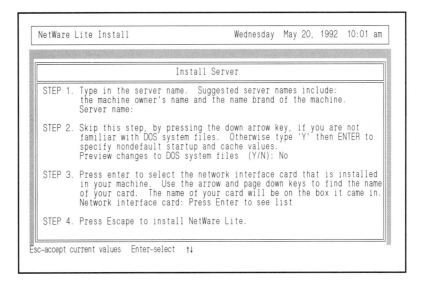

Entry of the server name

The server name is required for the later allocation of resources and must be specified. The maximum length of this name is 15 characters.

7.   Enter the name you want to use (for example, ACCOUNTING) and press the ⌈Enter⌉ key.

8.   The installation program checks whether or not the necessary system settings (FILES, BUFFERS) are in the CONFIG.SYS file. Step 2, in the INSTALL program, allows you to accept or change the NetWare Lite default values. If you would like to accept the default settings, simply press ⌈Enter⌉ to continue. If you would like to view or change the default settings, press ⌈Y⌉ and then press ⌈Enter⌉. The following screen will appear:

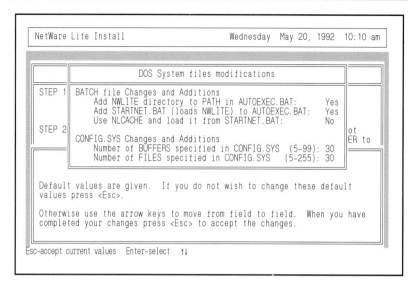

Default system settings

The entries will make the following changes to the system when it is booted.

Add NWLITE directory to PATH in AUTOEXEC.BAT

This will add the NetWare Lite directory to the PATH statement in the AUTOEXEC.BAT file. Adding the directory to the path starts NetWare Lite from any directory. If this change is not made, you will have to open the NWLITE directory (CD \NWLITE Enter) before you can run any of the NetWare Lite program files.

Add STARTNET.BAT (loads NWLITE) to AUTOEXEC.BAT

This option will allow you to load NetWare Lite when the computer is booted. If you allow this change, all necessary program files and network drivers will be loaded and you will be attached to the network automatically.

Use NLCACHE and load it from STARTNET.BAT

Novell has added a disk cache program to Version 1.1 of Netware Lite. This program can help improve the speed of the network by storing important file information in memory. The INSTALL program will make the default setting based on the configuration of the computer; it may be either "Yes" or "No".

☞   You should only use one disk cache program on the computer. If you are currently using another disk cache program (e.g., SMARTDRV or PCKWIK), you should either answer "No" at this prompt or remove the call to your other disk caching program and use the NetWare Lite cache.

Novell also recommends that a "lazy write" or "write behind" cache option be used only with NLCACHE. If you are using another disk cache program that has this capability, it should be disabled. Please see your documentation for further information.

Number of BUFFERS specified in CONFIG.SYS (5-99)

The buffers command refers to the way DOS manages input and output to and from the disk drives. NetWare Lite will run most efficiently with the number of BUFFERS set to 30.

Number of FILES specified in CONFIG.SYS (5-255)

This option will set the number of files DOS can have open at any given time. When using a database program, for example, you may need to open multiple files simultaneously. The default FILE setting is 30.

LASTDRIVE specified in CONFIG.SYS (H-Z)

If you are installing NetWare Lite in client or client/server mode, a LASTDRIVE option will also be shown. NetWare Lite will assign logical drives (mappings) to hard disks or directories on the file server. These drives, just like physical drives, are designated with letters.

The LASTDRIVE command will reserve letters so that they may be used with NetWare Lite. For example, if the workstation, as a stand-alone computer, has drives A:, B: and C:, then having the LASTDRIVE parameter set to M would leave letters D: through M: available for the network drive mappings. NetWare Lite requires at least two logical drives to enable it to be activated.

This means, for example, if the stand-alone computer has drives A:, B: and C:, then the LASTDRIVE entry in C:\CONFIG.SYS must be:

```
LASTDRIVE=E
```

The installation program suggests:

```
LASTDRIVE=M
```

In most cases you should press (Enter) to confirm this setting. The installation program then makes the required LASTDRIVE entry in the CONFIG.SYS file of the computer.

    If the computer is currently a workstation on a NetWare 2.x or 3.x network, the drive mappings for this network will be effected by the LASTDRIVE parameter. If the LASTDRIVE parameter is set to M, the login drive for the NetWare 2.x or 3.x network would become N:.

9.   You will then need to specify the type of network card that was installed in the computer. You should press (Enter) in Step 3, to see a list of the available choices. The available options will be listed as follows:

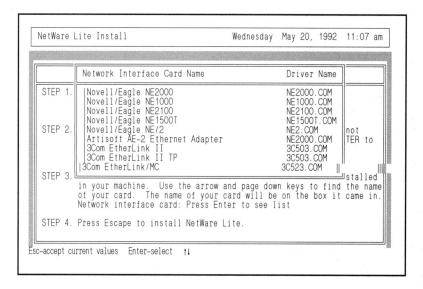

Designating the available network drivers

10.   Use the cursor keys to select the type of network card that was installed and press (Enter).

If your network card is not listed, you will have to select the *OTHER CARDS option (at the very bottom). You will then be asked to insert the driver disk that the manufacturer supplied with the card, and confirm it by pressing (Esc). A new list, containing the necessary driver, appears. You should highlight your selection and press (Enter) to continue.

11.   The selection of the driver causes the following screen to appear:

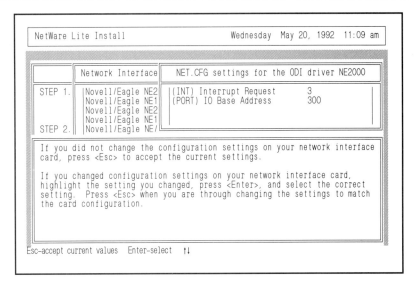

```
NetWare Lite Install                    Wednesday  May 20, 1992  11:09 am

         ┌──────────────┬──────────────────────────────────────────┐
         │ Network Interface │ NET.CFG settings for the ODI driver NE2000 │
 STEP 1. │ Novell/Eagle NE2 │ (INT) Interrupt Request         3        │
         │ Novell/Eagle NE1 │ (PORT) IO Base Address        300        │
         │ Novell/Eagle NE2 │                                          │
         │ Novell/Eagle NE1 │                                          │
 STEP 2. │ Novell/Eagle NE/ │                                          │
         └──────────────────┴──────────────────────────────────────────┘
    If you did not change the configuration settings on your network interface
    card, press <Esc> to accept the current settings.

    If you changed configuration settings on your network interface card,
    highlight the setting you changed, press <Enter>, and select the correct
    setting.  Press <Esc> when you are through changing the settings to match
    the card configuration.



Esc—accept current values   Enter—select   ↑↓
```

Interrupt selection

12.   In this window you must specify the interrupt request and IO
       base address settings that were set on the network card. If
       you did not change the settings before installing the network
       card, press Esc to accept the defaults (IRQ 3, IO base 300).

       If you changed the interrupt or IO base address settings on
       the network card, use the cursor keys to highlight the
       selection you changed and press Enter. You may then choose
       the correct option from the displayed list. You should press
       the Esc key to confirm the new settings.

       The selection of an interrupt and the corresponding address
       helps prevent possible hardware conflicts when the network
       card is in use. For this reason, it may be necessary to
       customize these entries to your own special needs. The
       settings you choose depend on the hardware installed in
       your computer.

       In the case of the available interrupt request (IRQ), the
       following assignments are valid:

       2   Graphics card (EGA/VGA)
       3   Interface COM2
       4   Interface COM1
       5   Interface LPT2
       6   Controller for floppy disk drive
       7   Interface for LPT1
       9   Identical with 2 (EGA/VGA)

The following assignments are also available on a 16-bit computer:

10 DCB3 controller
11 DCB controller
12 PS/2 mouse connection
14 Hard disk controller

From this list you can see that many of the system addresses may already be occupied. If you are unsure which addresses (IRQ) are still available for the network, you should first attempt to use the default set by the installation program. You will always have the option of changing these settings later.

13.   When all installation options have been set, press ⌈Esc⌋ to install the NetWare Lite software. The following screen informs you that the software has been successfully installed.

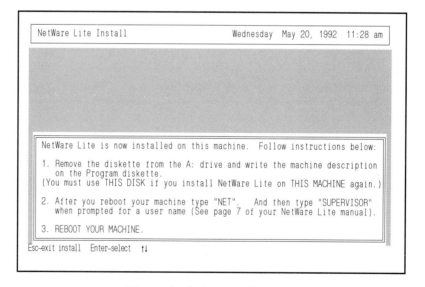

```
 NetWare Lite Install                      Wednesday  May 20, 1992  11:28 am



 ┌──────────────────────────────────────────────────────────────────────────┐
 │ NetWare Lite is now installed on this machine.  Follow instructions below: │
 │                                                                            │
 │ 1. Remove the diskette from the A: drive and write the machine description │
 │    on the Program diskette.                                                │
 │ (You must use THIS DISK if you install NetWare Lite on THIS MACHINE again.)│
 │                                                                            │
 │ 2. After you reboot your machine type "NET".   And then type "SUPERVISOR"  │
 │    when prompted for a user name (See page 7 of your NetWare Lite manual). │
 │                                                                            │
 │ 3. REBOOT YOUR MACHINE.                                                    │
 └──────────────────────────────────────────────────────────────────────────┘
 Esc-exit install   Enter-select   ↑↓
```

The end of the installation

To exit the installation procedure, you only need to press ⌈Esc⌋, which will return you to the operating system prompt.

The installation procedure is now complete.

2.3   After Installation

After completing the installation you should remove the NetWare Lite distribution diskette and reset the computer. The changes made to the AUTOEXEC.BAT and CONFIG.SYS files will take effect, and you will be ready to use NetWare Lite.

2.4   Changing the Network Cards

If the settings on the network card, or the network card itself, must be changed, NetWare Lite will have to be reinstalled to update the necessary drivers.

The procedure is identical with the "first time installation" of NetWare Lite. The only difference is that you will be reminded that NetWare Lite is already installed, if you have selected server mode. This reminder appears as follows:

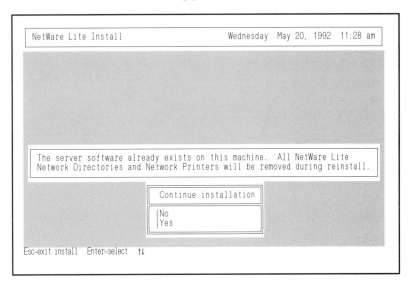

Replacement of the existing NetWare Lite version

If you confirm the new installation, you can continue, as previously described. You must remember to select the new card type or settings when given the option.

2.5   Working on a Workstation Without a Hard Disk

It's possible to include a workstation without a local hard disk in a Netware Lite network; a floppy drive must be available, however. You only need to create a start-up disk using the following steps:

1. First, place a new diskette in drive A: and format it as a system disk, using the following command:

    ```
    FORMAT A /S Enter
    ```

2. You must then copy the following files from the NetWare Lite program diskette to the boot diskette just created:

    ```
    LSL.COM
    IPXODI.COM
    CLIENT.EXE
    NET.EXE
    ```

3. In addition to these files, you must also copy a driver for the network card utilized. Since NetWare Lite has the most common drivers available on the program diskette, you should first find out which drivers are available. For the Novell/Eagle NE2000 network card the corresponding driver is called NE2000.COM. This driver, for example, is found on the Netware Lite program disk.

4. The next job is to create a CONFIG.SYS file on the start-up diskette that will establish the LASTDRIVE setting. Set up this file using a text editor or the DOS COPY command:

    ```
    COPY CON A:CONFIG.SYS Enter
    ```

    The computer will then wait for input, type in the following line:

    ```
    LASTDRIVE=M Enter
    ```

    End the file with:

    ```
    Ctrl Z + Enter
    ```

5. You should now create an AUTOEXEC.BAT file on the diskette; use a text editor or the DOS COPY command as follows:

    ```
    COPY CON A:AUTOEXEC.BAT Enter
    ```

   This example assumes you are using a Novell/Eagle NE2000 network card. You must substitute the driver for your network card on the NE2000 line.

Create the AUTOEXEC.BAT file with the entries that follow:

```
LSL Enter
NE2000 Enter
IPXODI A Enter
CLIENT Enter
NET LOGIN Enter
```

If you used the DOS COPY command, end the file with:

Ctrl Z +Enter

6.   When the indicated steps are complete, you will then be able to insert the start up disk into a workstation without a hard disk and boot the computer.

      If you are installing NetWare Lite in Client mode, on a computer without a hard disk and two floppy drives, you can use the install program to install NetWare Lite to the other floppy drive.

If you have done everything correctly, the workstation in question will boot and you will be asked to enter a user ID (NET LOGIN). Nothing more stands here in the way of utilizing NetWare Lite.

The procedure for starting a workstation, as previously described, will only work if there is at least one server active within the network at this time.

A workstation without a local hard disk should be assigned a network directory on one of the servers, where the DOS system files are stored. In this way you will have access to the necessary operating system commands of DOS, even from such a workstation.

Please note that the default value (Interrupt 3) for the network card driver is assumed. This can, under certain circumstances, lead to conflicts with the existing hardware.

2.6   NetWare Lite With a NetWare Network

In addition to accessing the file server and resources of the NetWare Lite network, you can also access a NetWare network. The advantage is that it's possible for the workstations on the NetWare network to access the local resources of another computer which is attached with NetWare Lite; this is not possible with NetWare 286 or 386. In some cases, such as a CD-ROM drive, this makes the installation much easier. Installing a CD-ROM drive in a NetWare file server can be very difficult. The drive can be easily installed in a workstation and shared with the use of NetWare Lite.

There are a few things that should be considered when using
NetWare and NetWare Lite together. A brief description of the
possible problems will be provided later.

The installation in a workstation is basically the same as the
installation in a single-user computer. The important thing to
remember is that you should use the same entries used to generate
the IPX file when specifying the interrupt addresses for NetWare
Lite.

Do not attempt to install NetWare Lite on a non-dedicated file
server; this could cause problems. NetWare Lite is designed
exclusively to be installed and run on the workstations.

Once the installation is complete, there are two methods by which
you can activate NetWare Lite in a NetWare network. It is
assumed that you want to use both the "big" versions of NetWare
and NetWare Lite simultaneously.

The important thing during activation is that you don't call both
the IPX.COM file and the IPXODI.COM file. These files serve the
same purpose and problems can result if they are both loaded.

Presented below are two files that can be used as start-up files:

```
IPX
NETX (or NET3, NET4, NET5)
SHARE
SERVER
CLIENT
```

The second form of a possible start-up file could appear as follows:

```
LSL
NE2000
IPXODI A
SHARE
SERVER
CLIENT
NETX (or NET3, NET4, NET5)
```

In both cases the necessary files and drivers are activated to allow
the simultaneous use of both NetWare (for example, 2.2 or 3.11)
and NetWare Lite. In the second example, the network driver for
the NE2000 network card was used. This must be changed to match
the network card installed in the workstation.

The case is similar with the SERVER.EXE and CLIENT.EXE files.
For example, the use of the server and the client modes are
assumed in the previous examples. If there is no need for both
modes, the corresponding entry can be omitted from the start file.

The LASTDRIVE entry in the CONFIG.SYS file on the NetWare Lite workstation will change the login drive on the "big" Network. For example, if the LASTDRIVE entry is set as follows:

```
LASTDRIVE=M
```

The login drive for the NetWare network will be N:.

3. NetWare Lite On The Server

Installing NetWare Lite is the first step on the way to an operational network. Afterwards, however, you will still have to make some system settings. This chapter will show you how to log into the network for the first time and set up the file server.

If you use NetWare Lite exclusively on a workstation in client mode, you can skip this chapter and go to Chapter 4. There you will find information on activating a workstation and using NetWare Lite.

3.1 Activating NetWare Lite on the Server

After installing NetWare Lite on the computer you are going to use as a server and rebooting the computer, you are ready to begin working with NetWare Lite.

3.1.1 Activating with STARTNET.BAT

To load NetWare Lite, you can use a special batch file that was generated during installation. This file, called STARTNET.BAT, contains the necessary program calls and also initializes the connection to the network by activating the network drivers.

To run STARTNET.BAT, you should change to the directory in which you installed NetWare Lite. This directory also contains the program files and the necessary network drivers.

If you installed NetWare Lite in server mode (Server or Client/Server), the files will be stored in a directory named C:\NWLITE. If you installed in client mode and specified a directory other than C:\NWLITE, you will have to change into that directory to run STARTNET.BAT. To change to the \NWLITE directory, type the following at the DOS prompt:

```
CD \NWLITE Enter
```

 If you expanded the path specification to include the NetWare Lite directory as described during installation, then you can start NetWare Lite from any directory. Simply type the following at the DOS prompt:

```
STARTNET Enter
```

In the next few paragraphs we're going to give you a look at the starting procedure and the files used.

STARTNET.BAT is a normal batch file, or collection of DOS commands. You can make any changes you want to the contents of this file and adapt it to your own needs. For example, if you change the network card the STARTNET.BAT file can be modified so that it loads the new driver.

The contents of this file varies from computer to computer, according to the different network cards used in the individual computers and the set mode (Server/Client).

Here's an example of what STARTNET.BAT could look like:

```
LSL
NE1000.COM
IPXODI A
SHARE
SERVER
CLIENT
```

The fastest way to view the contents of STARTNET.BAT is to use the TYPE command as follows:

```
TYPE STARTNET.BAT Enter
```

Here's what the different elements of STARTNET.BAT are:

LSL

Calling this program loads the Link-Support-Layer. This makes it possible to access the network driver that will be loaded next, and makes the connection between the transmission protocol (IPXODI) and the network card.

DRIVER.COM

After LSL, the network driver is loaded. This makes it possible to access and connect with the installed network card.

The name of the driver file appears in place of DRIVER. For example, an NE2000/EAGLE network card has a driver file called NE2000.COM.

It's also important that the driver is created for the Open-Data-Link-Interface (ODI). Only these drivers can be used with NetWare Lite. You can recognize this driver type by its file extension, either .COM or .EXE.

IPXODI A

This driver program (transmission protocol) controls all data exchange between the individual stations (nodes) of a network.

By specifying A, you load the first of three possible protocol options. This option is called Internetwork packet exchange protocol (IPX) and represents a standard in transmission protocols.

The following are the other two protocol options of IPXODI. However, you cannot use these options with NetWare Lite.

SPX   Sequenced internetwork packet exchange
DIAGNOSTICS   Internetwork diagnostics protocol

SHARE

This program is not a component of NetWare Lite, but instead is a program of the operating system being used. Activating this program enables file sharing and file locking in network or multitasking environments. The program must be loaded in order for the users of a network to share files.

NetWare Lite only requires that you install the SHARE program on a computer functioning as a server. A client computer doesn't need this specification.

SERVER

This program makes it possible to use the computer in server mode. This means that the server computer makes its resources (hard drives, printers etc.) available to other network users.

CLIENT

This program loads client mode to access the resources of other computers that were declared as servers.

NET.CFG

This file contains the network card options chosen during the installation of NetWare Lite. For example, if you are using a NE2000 card, with interrupt request 3 and I/O base address 300, the file would appear as:

```
# Setup the NE2000 card
Link driver NE2000

        INT 3
        PORT 300
```

If you change the settings on the card, you can simply change this
file rather than reinstalling NetWare Lite. If the settings on the
NE2000 card were changed to interrupt request 5 and I/O base
address 340, you could use a text editor to change the file to:

```
# Setup the NE2000 card
Link driver NE2000

        Int 5
        Port 340
```

☞   If you have any problems modifying this file, please
         remember that it can be recreated using the
         installation program.

To load NetWare Lite, all you have to do is call STARTNET.BAT
by typing the following:

STARTNET [Enter]

```
C:\NWLITE>LSL
NetWare Link Support Layer V1.20 (911120)
(C) Copyright 1990, 1991 Novell, Inc.  All Right Reserved.

C:\NWLITE>NE2000.COM
Novell NE2000 Ethernet MLID v1.34 (910603)
(C) Copyright 1991 Novell, Inc.  All Rights Reserved.

Int 5, Port 320, Node Address 1B1D92AB
Max Frame 1514 bytes, Line Speed 10 Mbps
Board 1, Frame Ethernet_802.3

C:\NWLITE>IPXODI
NetWare IPX Protocol v1.10 (911120)
(C) Copyright 1991 Novell, Inc.  All Rights Reserved

IPX protocol bound to NE2000 MLID Board #1.

C:\NWLITE>SHARE
SHARE installed

C:\NWLITE>SERVER
NetWare Lite Server - Version 1.1
Copyright (c) 1991, 1992 Novell Inc.  All Rights Reserved.

SERVER.EXE was loaded successfully.

C:\NWLITE>CLIENT
NetWare Lite Client - Version 1.1
Copyright (c) 1991, 1992 Novell Inc.  All Rights Reserved.
Client.EXE was loaded successfully.
```

Calling STARTNET.BAT

You could also call NetWare Lite by entering the individual entries in the STARTNET.BAT file.

After you call STARTNET.BAT, a number of messages appear on the screen as shown in the previous illustration:

An error message or a status report after calling STARTNET.BAT will, in most cases, indicate a problem. It could be because a driver was configured incorrectly or a defective network card.

In such cases, refer to the appendix of this book, where you will find thorough explanations of all possible status reports as well as solutions for the errors.

3.1.2   Activating directly after the computer starts

Besides activating the network with STARTNET.BAT, there's also a second option.

You can call the STARTNET.BAT file in the C:\AUTOEXEC.BAT file. This file is executed when the computer is started, so using a text editor to append the following line to the AUTOEXEC.BAT file will automatically start the network the next time you restart the computer:

```
C:\NWLITE\STARTNET
```

Below we'll give you an example of what an AUTOEXEC.BAT could look like when modified for this purpose. The lines with REM in front of them are only comments, and as such, are not necessary components of the file:

```
@ ECHO OFF
REM *****************************************************
REM ECHO OFF to suppress screen output
REM *****************************************************


REM *****************************************************
REM *      AUTOEXEC.BAT from NetWare Lite Step by Step   *
REM *      AUTOEXEC.BAT for the Server                   *
REM *****************************************************

REM *****************************************************
REM AN EXAMPLE OF A SEARCH PATH
REM *****************************************************
PATH C:\DOS;C:\BAT;C:\TOOLS;C:\NWLITE

REM *****************************************************
REM SET THE DOS PROMPT
REM *****************************************************
PROMPT $P$G
```

```
REM ***************************************************
REM CLEAR SCREEN
REM ***************************************************
@ CLS


REM ***************************************************
REM ACTIVATING FILES AND DRIVERS OF NETWARE LITE
REM ***************************************************

cd \NWLITE
call C:\NWLITE\STARTNET

REM ***************************************************
REM CLEAR SCREEN AND OUTPUT A MESSAGE
REM ***************************************************
@ CLS
@ ECHO   ***************************************************
@ ECHO   *                    SYSTEM STARTED               *
@ ECHO   *    Please enter your username to log in to the  *
@ ECHO   *              NetWare Lite network               *
@ ECHO   ***************************************************

REM ***************************************************
REM ENABLE LOGIN TO SYSTEM
REM ***************************************************
NET LOGIN

REM ******************* END OF FILE ********************
```

If you decide to use this sample file in your network, you do not have to include the lines of comment (REM). Also remember that many other system settings are made in the AUTOEXEC.BAT file. We suggest that you add the "Activating Files and Drivers of NetWare Lite" section to the end of your AUTOEXEC.BAT file, rather than replace your AUTOEXEC.BAT file with this example.

3.2   Logging In and Out On the Server

After activating NetWare, you must log in to the network before you can begin working.

3.2.1   Logging in on the Server for the first time

The process of logging in is necessary to gain access to the resources available on a network or perform any kind of activity on the network.

In NetWare Lite the process of logging in involves entering a username and password, if one has been assigned.

Each user has a different username. Only the supervisor (username: SUPERVISOR) has the right to assign and delete usernames. In addition to a username, the supervisor can also assign a password to a user. The user must then enter both the username and password each time he/she logs in on the system.

When installing NetWare Lite, the username SUPERVISOR is automatically assigned. This username is granted by default and cannot be changed. The supervisor is a user who controls the entire network. The username SUPERVISOR is not assigned a password; you must assign this after the installation.

The status of the supervisor

The username SUPERVISOR plays a special role in NetWare Lite. It's reserved for the person who monitors and controls the network. It's not possible to delete the name SUPERVISOR from the user list. In addition, only the SUPERVISOR has the right to assign or delete new usernames.

The only exception is assigning SUPERVISOR privileges to other network users. If a user is assigned supervisor privileges, then the user automatically has all the rights (and duties) of the SUPERVISOR. You can find more information on assigning SUPERVISOR privileges to network users in Chapter 5 of this book.

The username SUPERVISOR is automatically granted when you install NetWare Lite. Since the username SUPERVISOR has all the access options, you should quickly assign a password to this username. Only the supervisor (and his substitute) should know this password.

To log in on the system (as supervisor), type the following at the DOS prompt:

```
NET LOGIN  Enter
```

After a moment, you are prompted to enter a username. Type your username and press Enter. If the LASTDRIVE setting in the CONFIG.SYS file is not sufficient, you will see a status report after entering NET LOGIN.

You must have two available drives to run the NET utility. Increase LASTDRIVE in CONFIG.SYS and reboot, or delete drive mappings.

This message indicates that not enough drive letters are available using LASTDRIVE, in the CONFIG.SYS file. You should add the following line to your CONFIG.SYS file, if it has not already been added:

```
LASTDRIVE = M
```

With NetWare Lite V1.0, the installation program would add this line as an option. It is added automatically with NetWare Lite V1.1.

If the setting in the CONFIG.SYS is sufficient, you should enter the username:

```
SUPERVISOR Enter
```

When you type in usernames and passwords it doesn't matter whether you type them in uppercase or lowercase letters. You could also mix uppercase and lowercase letters.

For example, NetWare Lite treats the following three entries identically:

```
SUPERVISOR
supervisor
SuperVisor
```

This also applies to passwords.

After logging in as supervisor, you will see the following message on the screen:

```
You are logged in to the network as SUPERVISOR
```

You can log in to any server on the network by typing NET LOGIN.

To shorten the process for logging in, you can also specify the username following NET LOGIN, separated by a space. For example, you could also type:

```
NET LOGIN SUPERVISOR Enter
```

The result is the same; you are logged in to the system as SUPERVISOR.

3.2.2 Logging in using NET

NetWare Lite also has another method for logging in to the system. You could call the NET utility program after loading NetWare Lite by typing the following:

```
NET Enter
```

If NetWare Lite determines that you haven't logged in to the system yet, it prompts you to do this first. You will see the following status report on the screen:

```
You are not logged in. You must be logged in to run NET.
Type your username:
```

You cannot load NET until you enter your username and password, if you were assigned one.

This method of logging in is possible with most other NetWare Lite commands as well (see Chapter 13).

3.2.3   Logging off the system

After finishing your work as a user or supervisor, it is important to log out properly.

To log out, type NET LOGOUT from the DOS prompt, as shown in the following example:

```
NET LOGOUT  Enter
```

A message will appear indicating that you have logged out:

```
You have been logged out of the network.
```

However, the server still cannot be switched off. It's possible that other workstations (clients) will access this server.

To check, before you log out, type the following command:

```
NET ULIST  Enter
```

This provides you with a list of all users still logged in to the system.

3.3   Setting Up the Server

The first time you log in to the system as supervisor, you should make some important settings.

The following is a list of the settings:

• Assign a password for the supervisor.

• Assign names for the directories on the server that should be available to network users.

• Assign names for printers connected to the server that should be available in the network.

There are several other steps necessary for installing a complete network. For example, you must install usernames so that other network users can access the server. For more details refer to Chapter 5.

In the following examples, we assume that you have logged in to the system as supervisor.

3.3.1   Assigning a password for the supervisor

To define a password for the user SUPERVISOR, the following steps are necessary.

1.   Call NET by typing the following at the DOS prompt:

NET (Enter)

 If a "Bad command or file name" message appears when you call NET, then the NetWare Lite directory probably wasn't added to the search path in the AUTOEXEC.BAT file (see installation). In this case, change to the NWLITE directory and enter the command again, or place the directory name in front of the command as follows:

C:\NWLITE\NET (Enter)

When installing NetWare Lite V1.0, you were given an option to have the NWLITE directory automatically added to the path. With NetWare Lite V1.1, the NWLITE directory is automatically added to the path.

 When you call NET, if you are not logged in yet, NetWare Lite gives you the opportunity to do so by prompting you for a username and password, if one has been assigned.

After you call NET, the main menu appears, as shown in the following illustration:

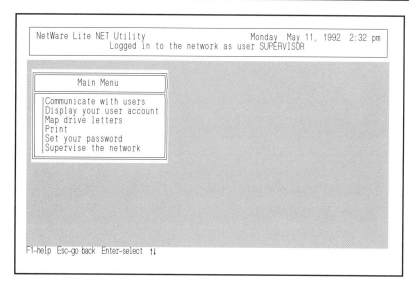

The main menu of NET

Before continuing, we'd like to present you with the following information about operating this program.

Working with NetWare Lite menus

There are two ways to select items from the various menus of NET. You can either press the first letter of the menu option (e.g., M for Map drive letters) or you can use the cursor keys. In either case you must confirm your selection with Enter. The Esc key can be used to move to the previous menu level. You can also use the Esc key from the main menu or Alt F10 to exit the program. The Ins and Del keys can be used to insert or delete an entry from a list.

If you need additional information in a certain menu, press F1. After that, you will see one or more Help screens. You can scroll up or down with PgUp and PgDn. When a help screen is active, press F1 again to receive a list of all possible key combinations and their functions in the NetWare Lite menus, as displayed in the following illustration:

```
 ┌────────────────────────────────────────────────────────────────────┐
 │ ┌────────────────────────────────────────────────────────────────┐ │
 │ │ NetWare Lite NET Utility              Monday  May 11, 1992  2:56 pm│ │
 │ │            Logged in to the network as user SUPERVISOR           │ │
 │ └────────────────────────────────────────────────────────────────┘ │
 │ ┌────────────────────────────────────────────────────────────────┐ │
 │ │ The function key assignments on your machine are:                │ │
 │ │                                                                  │ │
 │ │ ESCAPE        Esc            Back up to the previous level.       │ │
 │ │ ESCAPE        Alt F10        Exit the program.                    │ │
 │ │ CANCEL        F7             Cancel markings or edit changes.     │ │
 │ │ BACKSPACE     Backspace      Delete the character to the left of  │ │
 │ │                              the cursor.                          │ │
 │ │ INSERT        Ins            Insert a new item.                   │ │
 │ │ DELETE        Del            Delete an item.                      │ │
 │ │ MODIFY        F3             Rename/modify/edit the item.         │ │
 │ │ SELECT        Enter          Accept information entered or select │ │
 │ │                              the item.                            │ │
 │ │ HELP          F1             Provide on-line help.                │ │
 │ │ MARK          F5             Toggle marking for current item.     │ │
 │ │ CYCLE         Tab            Cycle through menus or screens.      │ │
 │ │ MODE          F9             Change Modes.                        │ │
 │ │ UP            Up arrow       Move up one line.                    │ │
 │ │ DOWN          Down arrow     Move down one line.                  │ │
 │ │ LEFT          Left arrow     Move left one position.             │ │
 │ └────────────────────────────────────────────────────────────────┘ │
 └────────────────────────────────────────────────────────────────────┘
```

Display of the available keys

Multiple selection in a list

When using NetWare Lite, there are many times when you'll have to make several selections from a particular list (e.g., when deleting a list of usernames). To do this, use the cursor keys to move the selection bar to the first item you want to select in the list. Then press F5. Move the selection bar to the next item and press F5 again. After selecting all of the desired items, simply execute the desired command. The command will be executed on all selected items.

A list can contain more items than can be displayed on the screen. The screen will automatically scroll up or down when the bar reaches the first or last item.

2.   To assign a password for the supervisor, you must first select *Set your password* from the main menu. To do this, simply press the S key and press Enter to confirm your selection.

     Keep in mind that when using *Set your password* you can only change the password of the user under the username you logged in. If you forget the password you will not be able to login again to change it.

To change the passwords of other users (as Supervisor), you must use a different method. For additional information refer to Chapter 5 of this book.

After selecting this menu item, a text box appears prompting you for the new password. You can choose any letters or numbers you want for the password.

3.   Enter the desired password and confirm your selection by pressing Enter.

☞   When you enter a password, it's not displayed on the screen. Think of this as an added safety feature, because someone could stand behind you and read your password to gain (unauthorized) access to the network.

☞   The principles   ernames also apply to passwords:
            It do   ther you type them in uppercase
                                    tters. The system automatically
                                 o uppercase letters.

                              r text box appears, as shown

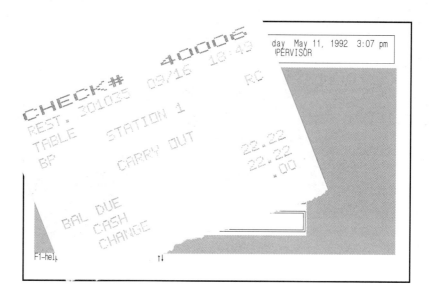

Retyping the password

4.   To be certain that you didn't make a mistake when you typed the password, you must retype it here (Retype new password:).

5.   After pressing Enter to confirm this entry, you return to the main menu of the NET program.

6.   Here you can exit the program by pressing [Alt] [F10] or [Esc], and answering Yes at the Exit Net prompt.

You have successfully set a password for username SUPERVISOR. The next time you log in to the network with this username, you will also be prompted to type this password.

Assigning a password to Supervisor

Necessary steps

```
NET [Enter]
Set your password [Enter]
Type password
Confirm by pressing [Enter]
Retype password
Confirm by pressing [Enter]
Press [Esc] or [Alt] [F10] to exit
```

3.3.2   Setting up network directories

You should name the resources of NetWare Lite so they are available on the network. The individual resources can then be accessed using these names.

In Chapter 4 of this book you will find out how to access the resources of a server from a workstation (client) on the network.

As you already know, the hard drive is one of the resources of a server. In NetWare Lite you have the option of breaking down a hard drive into directories. You can create a network directory by assigning a name to a directory on the server.

Before you begin assigning network directories, you must think about which directories of the server you want available.

Let's suppose that there is a directory called APPS on the hard drive C: (C:\APPS) of the current server. You want to prepare this directory for user access in the network. The following are the necessary steps:

1.   First, call the NET utilities program.

2.   Select *Supervise the network* from the main menu by highlighting this option and pressing [Enter]. After that, the following submenu appears on the screen:

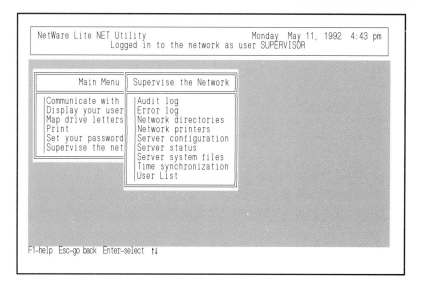

```
NetWare Lite NET Utility                    Monday  May 11, 1992  4:43 pm
                     Logged in to the network as user SUPERVISOR

    ┌─────────────────┐┌──────────────────────┐
    │   Main Menu     ││ Supervise the Network │
    ├─────────────────┤├──────────────────────┤
    │Communicate with ││Audit log             │
    │Display your user││Error log             │
    │Map drive letters││Network directories   │
    │Print            ││Network printers      │
    │Set your password││Server configuration  │
    │Supervise the net││Server status         │
    └─────────────────┘│Server system files   │
                       │Time synchronization  │
                       │User List             │
                       └──────────────────────┘




 F1-help  Esc-go back  Enter-select  ↑↓
```

The Supervise the network menu

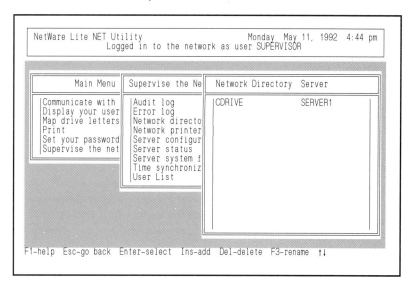

```
NetWare Lite NET Utility                    Monday  May 11, 1992  4:44 pm
                     Logged in to the network as user SUPERVISOR

  ┌─────────────────┐┌──────────────┐┌─────────────────────────────┐
  │   Main Menu     ││ Supervise the Ne ││ Network Directory   Server │
  ├─────────────────┤├──────────────┤├─────────────────────────────┤
  │Communicate with ││Audit log     ││CDRIVE          SERVER1       │
  │Display your user││Error log     ││                              │
  │Map drive letters││Network directo││                              │
  │Print            ││Network printer││                              │
  │Set your password││Server configur││                              │
  │Supervise the net││Server status ││                              │
  └─────────────────┘│Server system f││                              │
                     │Time synchroniz││                              │
                     │User List     ││                              │
                     └──────────────┘│                              │
                                     │                              │
                                     └─────────────────────────────┘

 F1-help  Esc-go back  Enter-select  Ins-add  Del-delete  F3-rename  ↑↓
```

Display of the available network directories

3. From this menu, select the item called *Network directories*.
    A window showing the available network directories will
    be displayed, as previously shown. If you have just installed
    NetWare Lite, you will only see the default, CDRIVE.

    During installation, CDRIVE is automatically assigned as a
    network directory. This name refers to the root directory of
    hard drive C:, making it possible to access the entire hard
    drive (including subdirectories).

This is a default which you can delete at any time. Simply highlight this name and press Del. If you answer Yes to the *Delete Network Directory* prompt, the directory will be removed from the list.

4.   To define a new network directory, first press Ins. A list of the servers available in the network appears, allowing you to set up network directories on any server you wish:

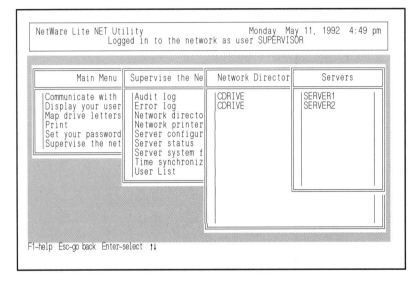

Display of the available servers

5.   Select the name of the server for which you want to assign a network directory. After selecting the server, you will be prompted for the name of the network directory. The name can use any combination of letters and numbers. A maximum of 15 characters in length can be used. This is the name that will be used by the workstations (clients), so be sure to make it a meaningful name.

6.   Enter the name (e.g., APPS_S1) and confirm it by pressing Enter.

     In this case, we added S1 to the name to refer to the server on which the directory exists. This should indicate that this network directory is on Server 1.

After entering the network directory name, you will be required to enter the actual name of the directory, including the path, and also assign the access rights users will have to this network directory.

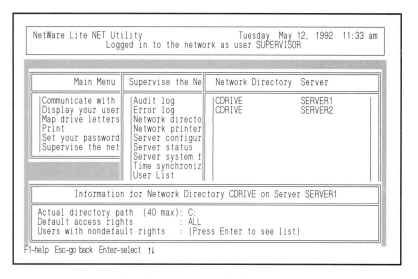

Setting a network directory

7. To do this, highlight the *Actual directory path* prompt and press Enter. You will then be given a cursor to enter the actual directory name as it exists on the server (e.g., C:\APPS) and confirm it by pressing Enter.

 If the directory is on a drive other than C:, you can use the Backspace key to delete C: and enter the new drive letter (e.g., D:\APPS).

After entering the actual directory name, you must define the Default access rights to the directory.

Access rights under NetWare Lite

The term "Access right" is a special setting which you will only encounter in networks or multi-station systems.

Access rights define the type of file access the individual users of the network will have. For example, the supervisor could determine that the users can only read certain files and cannot make changes.

NetWare Lite provides the following access rights when you assign network directories:

ALL

Allows unrestricted access to the files of the specified directory. Users can read, delete, execute and even make changes to files.

This is the highest priority level of access rights for file directories.

NONE

No access is allowed.

READ

This access right allows files to only be read and not changed or deleted.

8.   As a default, ALL access rights will be given. To change the access rights to NONE or READ, highlight ALL and press [Enter]. The following screen display will then allow you to select the desired option.

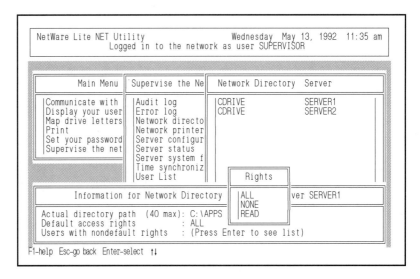

Selection of access rights

9.   Simply assign all access rights (ALL) for each new network directory. You can always change the rights later.

The definition of access rights in the Default access rights box is general (i.e., every user in the network receives these access rights).

You can define default access rights and individual access rights. You use the last option, *Users with nondefault rights* to assign an individual user different access rights.

10.   Since we have not defined any usernames yet, we will skip this step. Press [Esc] to end the input and answer Yes when

asked if you would like to save the changes. Chapter 6 will give a full example of setting nondefault access rights.

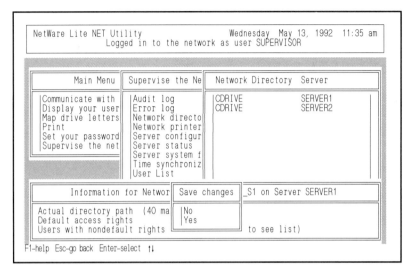

Saving the network directory information

You have just created a new network directory by assigning a name to a file directory of the server.

11.   Create more network directories or exit NET by pressing (Esc) or (Alt) (F10) and answering the *Exit NET* with Yes.

After you finish defining network directories, you have completed the first step toward making the directories of a server accessible to other users. In Chapter 4 you will find the steps necessary for a workstation (client) to access these network directories.

Setting up a network directory

```
NET (Enter)
Supervise the network (Enter)
Network directories (Enter)
Press (Ins)
Select the name of desired server
Confirm by pressing (Enter)
Type a name for the new network directory
Confirm by pressing (Enter)
Specify drive letter and actual path to the directory
Confirm by pressing (Enter)
Specify access rights
Confirm by pressing (Enter)
Press (Esc)
Press (Alt) (F10) and answer Exit NET with Yes to exit
```

3.3.3   Setting up network printers

Along with setting up network directories, you must also set up the network printers. The procedure is similar to the one for setting up network directories. Here you assign names that users will need to access a network printer.

The difference between local printers and network printers

When you connect a printer to a stand-alone computer and address this printer from DOS or an application program, you usually don't have to think about how an individual print job will be handled until the job is printed out; the operating system is in charge of this.

However, it's a little different when you use NetWare Lite. The operating system requires additional information, which makes it clear how incoming print jobs are to be processed. For the user, nothing changes when an application program is used. The print job can be sent in the same manner as a stand-alone computer.

In a network you must distinguish between network printers and local printers. A local printer is exactly the same as the printer you would use on a stand-alone computer. A network printer will be attached to a file server and shared by all network users. The sharing of resources, both printer and data, is one of the biggest advantages of a network.

The different workstations send their print jobs to the network printer. The print jobs are placed in a queue and then processed by the system (i.e., the incoming jobs are stored and processed sequentially and sent to the printer).

However, before you can use a printer attached to a server as a network printer, you must make specific settings. By making these settings the printer becomes available for other network users. Here are the necessary steps:

1.   First call the NET utility program by typing the following at the DOS prompt:

         NET Enter

2.   In the NET main menu, select the *Supervise the network* option. Use the cursor keys to do this, and then confirm your choice by pressing Enter.

3.   Select the *Network printers* option from the next menu.

Another window showing the network printers that have been defined will then appear. If you have not defined a network printer yet, this window will be empty.

4.   Press [Ins], which causes the following display to appear:

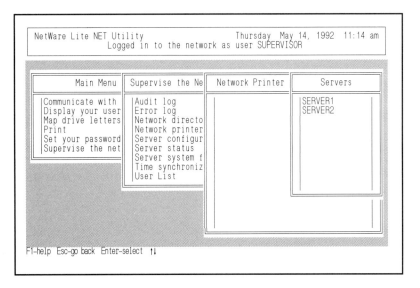

Display of the available servers

You can install network printers on any server you want. This allows you to be extremely flexible when you configure to make the existing resources available.

5.   From the list of available servers select the name of the server to which the printer, which will be used as a network printer, is connected. Use the cursor keys to select the desired server and press [Enter].

You must then specify a name for the network printer. It can be any combination of letters and numbers. The name is limited to 15 characters, similar to network directories.

You use this name to assign the network printer to the workstations (clients). You can read more about this in Chapter 4.

6.   Type a meaningful name (e.g., LASER_S1) and confirm the selection by pressing [Enter].

     In the previous example, we added S1 to the name to indicate that the printer is connected to Server 1.

After confirming the entry, the following screen display will appear:

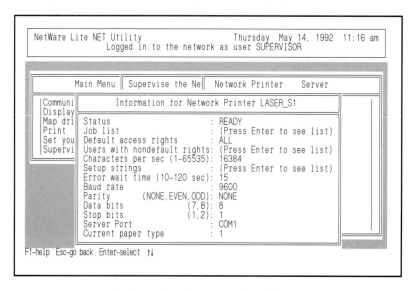

Selection of printer port

7.   Next, you must define the port to which the printer is connected. Many times the first printer of a computer is connected to the LPT1 port (first parallel port). Since LPT1 is the default specification here, if your printer is attached to LPT1, simply press Enter. After defining the printer port, you will see the following screen display:

Settings for the network printer

In this window you can make some settings for the network printer. For example, you can define control characters for printer initialization. You can also determine which users are allowed access to the network printer.

Status

Specifies the current status of the network printer, with several possible alternatives: e.g., READY (printer ready to receive) or PAUSED (printer output interrupted).

Job list

When you select this item, the print jobs currently waiting to print are displayed.

Default access rights

Display of the default access rights for the selected printer.

Users with nondefault rights

Displays a list of the individual access rights for the selected printer. These are rights assigned to individual users which differ from general access rights.

Characters per second (1-65535)

You can increase the speed of printer output by specifying the number of characters printed per second.

Setup strings

Lets you specify a control sequence for printer initialization.

Error wait time (10-120 Sec)

Lets you specify a time period (in seconds) that the server will wait before indicating a printing error. If you have trouble printing to a laser printer, try increasing this setting.

Server port

Specifies the port to which the network printer is connected.

Current paper type

Defines the type of paper currently in the printer.

If your printer is connected to a serial port (COM1 or COM2), you will also see the following:

Baud rate

Specifies the baud rate or data transfer rate (Bit/second) at which the data is sent to the printer.

Parity (NONE, EVEN, ODD)

Set the desired parity here. This is the method used to detect data transmission errors.

Data bits

Specifies the number of data bits in a character; the default is 8.

Stop bits

Specifies the number of stop bits used to signal the end of a character; the default setting is 1.

Usually, it will not be necessary to change the default values.

8.   Press (Esc) to exit this window. The newly defined printer will then appear in the list of available network printers, as shown in the following illustration:

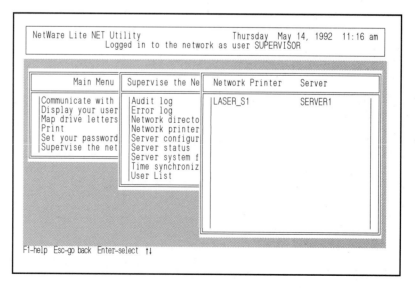

Display of the newly set network printer

9.   Here you have the opportunity to define other network printers or exit the NET program by pressing (Esc) or (Alt) (F10).

This is the last important setting that a supervisor should make initially. In Chapter 4 of this book we will provide the necessary steps to access the network printers and directories from a workstation (client).

Setting up network printers

Necessary steps

```
NET [Enter]
Supervise the network [Enter]
Network printers [Enter]
Press [Ins]
Select the desired server [Enter]
Type a name for the new network printer
Confirm by pressing [Enter]
Select the printer port [Enter]
Make any printer specific settings
Press [Esc] to exit and save changes
```

4.   Setting Up A Workstation (Client)

Setting up a network under NetWare Lite involves more than simply installing NetWare Lite on the server. After installation, the connected workstations must be configured and prepared for use in the network.

This requires NetWare Lite to be installed on the workstation in question (see Chapter 2). Keep in mind that you can only use a computer as a client (workstation), if you selected either Client or Client/Server mode during installation.

4.1   Activating NetWare Lite On a Workstation

Although the procedure for activating NetWare Lite on a client (workstation) is similar to activating it on a server, we'll discuss it separately here.

Before you start a workstation to connect with the servers and workstations connected to the network, the following requirements must be met:

1.   The workstation must be connected with the server and the other workstations by a network card and cable.

2.   The computer that's used as a client must have a separate version of NetWare Lite installed on it.

3.   NetWare Lite must be loaded on the server that's accessed. Although it's not necessary for anyone to be logged in to the server, the necessary program files and network driver (STARTNET.BAT) should be active.

After these requirements are met a computer can be used as a workstation (client). Then you can begin working on the workstation. Your first task is to activate NetWare Lite.

4.1.1   Activating with STARTNET.BAT

A workstation has a special start file called STARTNET.BAT. This start file is stored in the directory in which NetWare Lite was installed. This is also where the program files and network drivers for NetWare Lite are located.

After booting the workstation, you must first change to the directory in which you installed NetWare Lite. For example, if

you installed NetWare Lite into the directory C:\NWLITE, type
the following at the DOS prompt:

CD \NWLITE [Enter]

     If you only installed NetWare Lite in client mode,
then you can have the files placed in any file
directory that you specify during installation.
Otherwise (server or client/server mode) the
NetWare Lite files are always in a file directory
named \NWLITE.

If you added the NetWare Lite directory to the search
path, as described in the chapter on installation, you
can start NetWare Lite from any directory.

You can load NetWare Lite by typing the following at the DOS
prompt:

STARTNET [Enter]

```
C:\NWLITE>LSL
NetWare Link Support Layer v1.20 (911120)
(C) Copyright 1990, 1991 Novell, Inc. All Rights Reserved.

Max Boards 4, Max Stacks 4

C:\NWLITE>NE2000.COM
Novell NE2000 Ethernet MLID v1.34 (910603)
(C) Copyright 1991 Novell, Inc. All Rights Reserved.

Int 5, Port 320, Node Address 1B1D92AB
Max Frame 1514 bytes, Line Speed 10 Mbps
Board 1, Frame ETHERNET_802.3

C:\NWLITE>IPXODI A
NetWare IPX Protocol v1.20 (911120)
(C) Copyright 1990, 1991 Novell, Inc. All Rights Reserved.

IPX protocol bound to MLID Board #1.

C:\NWLITE>SHARE
SHARE installed

C:\NWLITE>CLIENT
NetWare Lite Client - Version 1.1
Copyright (C) 1991, 1992 Novell, Inc. All Rights Reserved.
```

Calling STARTNET.BAT

You could also call NetWare Lite by typing the individual entries contained in STARTNET.BAT. However, using STARTNET.BAT is much easier.

After activating NetWare Lite, messages appear on the screen as shown in the previous display:

 If error messages or status reports appear after you call STARTNET.BAT, then there is a problem somewhere. It could be because of a defective driver, a defective network card, or something similar.

In such cases, refer to the appendix of this book, where you will find detailed explanations on all possible status reports and suggestions for correcting the errors.

4.1.2 Activating NetWare Lite automatically

You can also activate NetWare Lite on a workstation automatically after startup. Simply add the necessary calls to the start file of the computer. Under DOS, the start file is called AUTOEXEC.BAT. This file must either be in the root directory of the first hard drive (C:) or on the boot diskette, if you start the workstation with a diskette.

Add a call to the STARTNET.BAT file to the end of your AUTOEXEC.BAT file. As soon as you restart the computer, NetWare Lite is automatically activated and immediately available to you.

The following is what a modified AUTOEXEC.BAT file could look like:

```
@ ECHO OFF
REM ****************************************************
ECHO OFF will suppress screen output
REM ****************************************************
REM AUTOEXEC.BAT from NetWare Lite Step by Step
REM Used as AUTOEXEC.BAT for the client (workstation)
REM ****************************************************

REM ****************************************************
REM DEFINITION OF A SEARCH PATH
REM ****************************************************
PATH C:\DOS;C:\BAT;C:\NWLITE


REM ****************************************************
REM DEFINITION OF THE SYSTEM PROMPT
REM ****************************************************
```

```
PROMPT $P$G


REM ********************************************************
REM CLEAR SCREEN
REM ********************************************************
@ CLS
REM ********************************************************
REM ACTIVATE NETWARE LITE FILES AND DRIVERS
REM ********************************************************
CD \NWLITE
STARTNET


REM ********************************************************
REM CLEAR SCREEN AND OUTPUT A MESSAGE
REM ********************************************************
@ CLS
@ ECHO  **************************************************
@ ECHO *                SYSTEM STARTED                    *
@ ECHO *    Please enter your username to log             *
@ ECHO *     into the NetWare Lite network                *
@ ECHO  **************************************************


NET LOGIN

REM ****************************************** END OF FILE
```

If you decide to use this sample file at your workstation, you could
omit the lines of comment (REM). Also remember that many system
settings are made in the AUTOEXEC.BAT file. We suggest that
you add the section of the example, beginning with the "Activate
NetWare Lite Files and Drivers" section, rather than replace your
AUTOEXEC.BAT file with this example.

4.2   Logging In and Out at a Workstation

After loading NetWare Lite, you can begin working with the
network immediately.

4.2.1   Logging in at a workstation (client)

Before you can access the resources of a network from a
workstation, you must first log in to the network.

      To log in to a network, you need a username. Each user
gets his/her own username.

Each user can also be assigned a password which must be specified
each time the network is logged in.

If you haven't been assigned a username yet, you should contact your network supervisor. Only the supervisor has the right to assign or delete usernames.

After activating NetWare Lite, log in to the network by typing the following at the DOS prompt:

    NET LOGIN [Enter]

You will then be prompted for your username:

    Type username:

Type your assigned username and confirm it by pressing [Enter].

 If no server has been activated in the network at the time you log in, a message appears on the screen, informing you of this. In this case, you must first make sure that a server is loaded, which the workstation (client) can access.

If you were assigned a password, you will be prompted for it next. The following message appears on the screen:

    Type password:

You should then enter your password and confirm it by pressing [Enter].

After typing the username and password, you are ready to work in NetWare Lite.

 After successfully installing NetWare Lite on a workstation, you are automatically provided with the username SUPERVISOR. This username should be reserved exclusively for the network supervisor.

When you enter usernames and passwords, it doesn't matter if you type them in uppercase or lowercase letters. You can also mix uppercase and lowercase letters:

    SUPERVISOR
    supervisor
    SUPERvisor

These three different entries function the same.

After logging in, you will see a message on the screen similar to the following:

```
Logged in to the network as SUPERVISOR
```

You can shorten the process of logging in by specifying the username directly after NET LOGIN, as follows:

```
NET LOGIN SUPERVISOR [Enter]
```

4.2.2 Logging in with the NET utility

Besides NET LOGIN, there is also another way to log in to the network.

You could call the NET utility program right after loading NetWare Lite, by typing the following:

```
NET [Enter]
```

When NetWare Lite notices that you haven't logged in to the network yet, it prompts you to do so. After entering your username and password, you move to the NET utility program and are logged in to the network.

4.2.3 Logging out from the system

Just as you must log in to work in the network, you must also log out when you're finished working. Make sure you log out properly before switching off a workstation.

To log out, use the NET LOGOUT command, as shown in the following example:

```
NET LOGOUT [Enter]
```

Then you receive a message informing you that the logging out process has been performed:

```
You have been logged out of the network
```

This tells you that you have logged out and can now switch off the workstation.

4.3 Using Network Directories

After logging in, there are two important settings you must make before working at a workstation. These settings make it possible for the workstation (client) to use the workstation.

The following are the settings:

- Assign drive names for the installed network directories on the server.

- Assign the network printers to be used by the workstation (client).

You must log in to the network before making the settings described in the next section.

4.3.1   Assigning network directories

We have already stated that one of the basic principles of NetWare Lite, sharing resources, is possible by assigning names to the resources. The resources can then be accessed by the workstation, using these network names.

The hard drive or hard drives used in the server are also among these resources. The hard drive is organized according to the directories that are used.

So, you can assign a network name to the directories that should be available to the network users (Network directories).

  For more information on how to assign network directories (as the supervisor) refer to Chapter 3.

Remember that this assignment is a requirement for the following explanations. If you haven't assigned any network directories to the server, then you won't be able to assign any to a workstation.

The following steps are necessary for assigning network directories:

1.   Call the NET utility program by typing the following at the DOS prompt:

     NET (Enter)

  You will use NET to make most of the settings and definitions used on the network.

If you receive a status report when you call NET, you probably didn't add the NetWare Lite directory to the search path in the AUTOEXEC.BAT file (see chapter on installation).

Change to the directory in which you installed NetWare Lite (e.g., NWLITE). Type the command again, or place the name of

the directory in front of the command (e.g., \NWLITE\NET
[Enter]).

After you call NET, the main menu appears, as shown in the
following figure:

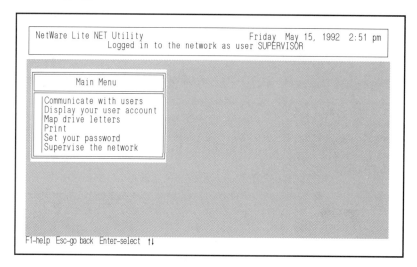

```
NetWare Lite NET Utility                    Friday  May 15, 1992  2:51 pm
                   Logged in to the network as user SUPERVISOR


          ┌─────────────────────────────┐
          │         Main Menu           │
          ├─────────────────────────────┤
          │ Communicate with users      │
          │ Display your user account   │
          │ Map drive letters           │
          │ Print                       │
          │ Set your password           │
          │ Supervise the network       │
          └─────────────────────────────┘




 F1-help  Esc-go back  Enter-select  ↑↓
```

The NET main menu

Operating the NetWare Lite menus

There are two ways to select items from the various menus of NET:

Either press the first letter of the menu item or, if several items of
the same menu start with the same letter, press the first letters of
the menu option (e.g., [S] [U] for *Supervise the Network*).

Another possibility is to use the cursor keys, with which you can
move the selection bar up and down within the menu. After
highlighting the item, press [Enter].

You can return to the previous menu (window) at any time by
pressing [Esc]. If you are in the main menu, you can exit the program
by pressing [Esc] and confirming the Exit prompt with Yes.

You can also exit the program by pressing the key sequence [Alt] [F10].
Pressing this key sequence automatically exits the program,
regardless of where you are in it.

Use [Ins] and [Del] to add an entry to a list ([Ins]) or remove an existing
entry from the list ([Del]).

If you need additional information in a certain menu, press [F1]. By
doing this, one or more Help screens will appear. You can scroll up
or down within the help screen using [PgDn] and [PgUp].

When a help screen is active, press F1 again to receive a list of all possible key combinations.

Multiple selection in a list

In numerous places within NET you can select several entries from a list. For example, you have this option when deleting several user names (more on this later). You can make a multiple selection with NetWare Lite so that you don't have to select each username individually.

To do this, simply highlight the first username and press F5. Then move the highlight to the next username and press F5 again. After selecting all the usernames, you can perform the desired action, which will affect all the names you selected.

Sometimes a list has more entries than will fit on the screen. In this case, as soon as you move the selection bar to the top or bottom of the menu, the screen will scroll to display the additional entries.

2.   Next, select *Map drive letters* in the NET main menu. To do this, use the cursor keys to move the selection bar to this item and press Enter.

The drive names currently available are displayed in an additional window, as shown in the next figure:

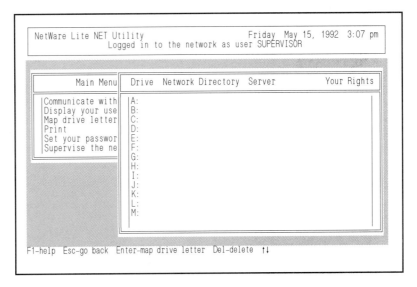

Display of available drive names

The number of available drive letters depends on which LASTDRIVE entry was made in the CONFIG.SYS file.

The NetWare Lite installation program will set this entry to M (this was an option with Version 1.0). So, you can use drive letters A: to M: for assigning network directories.

3.   First, you must determine which drive letter to map (or assign) to a network directory. To do this, move the selection bar to the desired drive letter and confirm by pressing [Enter].

   You could even use all the drive letters for mapping to network directories, including the drive letters for the local drives (e.g., A:).

However, we don't recommend doing this, since it blocks access to the local drives (or hard drives). Mapping a network directory takes precedence over using local drives (hard drives).

   The drive letter assignments are cancelled when you log out of the network or cancel the mapping.

After selecting the desired drive name you will see a list of the available network directories:

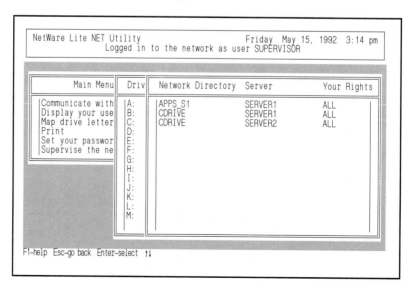

Display of the available network directories

The display of available network directories is
confined to those servers currently active in the
network.

During installation, each server is automatically mapped, as you
can see in the previous figure. The mapping is called CDRIVE.
This assignment refers to the root directory of hard drive C:,
making it possible to access the entire hard drive (including all
subdirectories).

As the supervisor, you can delete this default at any time. We
strongly suggest you do this.

4.   Choose the desired directory from the list by moving the
      selection bar to it and then press `Enter` to confirm it.

      The selected directory then appears in the list of drive
      names, as shown in the following illustration:

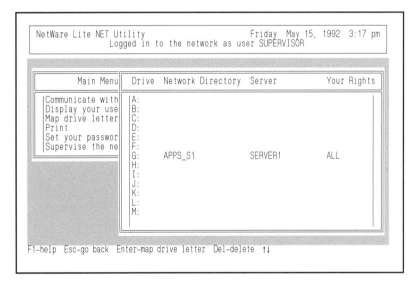

After mapping a network directory

5.   Now you can assign other network directories or exit the
      NET program by pressing `Alt` `F10` and answering Yes to the
      prompt that follows.

You have just mapped some network directories and made them
available for use (access). You can now access this directory on the
server using the drive letter that you assigned.

As soon as you make it possible for a user to access a certain directory of a hard drive, by making it a network directory, the user also has access to any subdirectories of this file directory.

Mapping network directories

Necessary steps

```
NET [Enter]
Map drive letters [Enter]
Choose drive letter
Confirm by pressing [Enter]
Select desired network directory
Confirm by pressing [Enter]
[Alt] [F10] and exit
```

4.3.2   Assigning network directories at DOS level

Before we show you how to access network directories, we'd like to show you another way of assigning network directories to a workstation.

Along with assigning network directories with the NET utility program, you can also use a command at the DOS prompt. NetWare Lite provides a command for this purpose called NET MAP.

NetWare Lite also provides you with a number of commands that partially fulfill the same tasks as certain menu items of the NET program.

Chapter 13 of this book provides detailed information about the NetWare Lite commands.

When you use NET MAP, specify the desired drive name, the network directory and the server where the directory is located.

For example, the following command:

```
NET MAP G: APPS_S1 SERVER_1 [Enter]
```

assigns drive letter G: to the network directory named APPS_S1. This network directory is on the server called SERVER_1.

The following message will also appear on the screen:

```
Drive G is mapped to Network Directory APPS_S1 on Server
SERVER_1.
```

4.3.3   Accessing network directories

After assigning a network directory to a workstation (client), you probably want to know how to access it. Nothing could be easier.

To access a mapped network directory, change to the drive letter that was assigned. For example, if you assigned the letter G: to a directory, then type the following:

```
G: Enter
```

This takes you to (logical) drive G:, which is the same directory defined on the server (see Chapter 3).

You can move freely in this directory (and its subdirectories) as though it were a directory on your computer.

    The type of access to a network directory is controlled by access rights in NetWare Lite. For additional information see Chapter 3 and Chapter 6 of this book.

4.3.4   Permanent assignment

Mapping network directories is only temporary. In other words, the network directories you define are only valid for the time you are logged in to the network.

Therefore, we recommend placing the necessary specifications in a batch file that can be run to enable the necessary settings.

The following is an example of what the batch file might look like:

```
REM ****************************************************
REM MAPDRV.BAT from NetWare Lite Step by Step
REM Batch file for assigning network
REM directories to a workstation (client)
REM ****************************************************


REM ****************************************************
REM MAPPING NETWORK DIRECTORIES
REM ****************************************************
NET MAP F: DATABASE SERVER_1
NET MAP G: TEXT SERVER_2
NET MAP H: GAMES SERVER_2


REM ****************************************************
```

```
REM CLEAR SCREEN AND OUTPUT A MESSAGE
REM *********************************************
@ CLS
@ ECHO   *********************************************
@ ECHO   ********** MAPPING SUCCESSFUL ******************
@ ECHO   *********************************************


REM *********************************************
REM DISPLAY MAPPING
REM *********************************************
NET MAP


REM *************************************** END OF FILE
```

You will find three assignments for network directories in this
sample file. The directories are called DATABASE, TEXT and
GAMES, which are all stored on different servers.

With NetWare Lite Version 1.1, you can also use the NET SAVE
command to automatically create a batch file, named
NLLOGIN.BAT. This batch file, which will be placed in the root
directory of the C: drive (C:\), can be run to log you in to the
network and set up the drive mappings and network printer
assignments. Use the NET SAVE command from the DOS prompt
as follows:

    NET SAVE [Enter]

The following message will be displayed to inform you that the
settings were saved successfully:

    Your network and environment settings were saved to
    NLLOGIN.BAT.

You can now call the NLLOGIN.BAT file to automatically log you
in to the network and set up the network drives. After running
STARTNET.BAT, use the following command to run
NLLOGIN.BAT:

    C:\NLLOGIN [Enter]

4.3.5   Displaying directory assignments

You can use the NET MAP command to display a list of all current
network drives.

Type the following command at the DOS prompt:

    NET MAP [Enter]

A list of the current network drive mappings will be displayed, similar to the following:

```
                         Current drive assignments
      Drive Letter:     Network directory   Server          Your Rights
      ============      =================   ============    ============

          F:            DATABASE_S1         SERVER_1        ALL
          G:            TEXT                SERVER_1        ALL
          H:            GAMES               SERVER_1        ALL
```

You can display this list at any time to find out which network directories are currently assigned to the workstation (client). You can receive information about the drive names, the assigned network directories, the server and the assigned access rights.

4.4 Using Network Printers

In Chapter 3 we already pointed out that using network printers, along with setting up network directories, is one of the most important options of a NetWare Lite networks.

By making certain assignments, you can access a printer from any workstation (client) that is connected to another computer (server).

The only requirement is that the computer (server), to which the printer is connected, be linked to the network and that the printer be defined as a network printer on this server.

Chapter 3 describes how to define a network printer for a server. Our discussion in this chapter is limited to assigning and accessing a network printer with a workstation (client).

4.4.1 Assigning network printers

Before you can access a network printer from a workstation (client), the following steps are required:

1. Load the NET utility program at the DOS prompt by typing the following:

    NET [Enter]

2. Then select *Print* in the NET main menu. The following screen display appears:

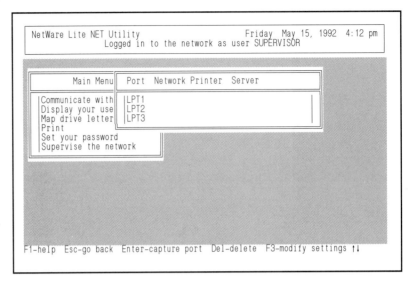

Display of the available ports

The printer ports of the workstation (client) are displayed. You must select the port whose printer output you want sent to the network printer. For example, to send all printer output to LPT1 (first parallel port) to a certain network printer, you would pick LPT1 from the list.

3.   To select a port, you must move the selection bar to the port name (e.g., LPT1) and press (Enter).

    When selecting the port, remember that by doing this, you are "shutting down" any connected local printer. As long as the assignment of the network printer is valid, you cannot access the (local) printer in any way.

This is comparable to giving drive names when mapping network directories. If you use names for local drives, you are blocking access to these (local) drives.

Also, in NetWare Lite you can never redirect the output to a serial port (COM1, COM2) at a workstation (client).

After selecting the port, a list of the (currently) available network printers appears, as shown in the following figure.

    This is a list of those network printers currently defined on the active server as network printers.

Use the name assigned to the printer on the server to assign a
network printer to a workstation (client). You can read more about
this later in this chapter.

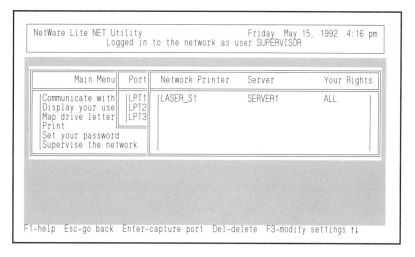

Display of the available network printers

4.   Now select the network printer to which you want to
      redirect printer output by placing the highlight on the name
      and confirming with ⌜Enter⌟. After confirming your selection,
      the following screen display will appear:

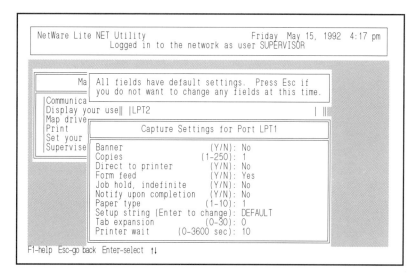

Defining the printer configuration

In the window that appears, you can make printer settings. For
example, you can specify whether to use a form feed, or how many
copies to print.

Since NetWare Lite automatically uses certain default settings, in most cases you will not have to worry about changing these printer settings.

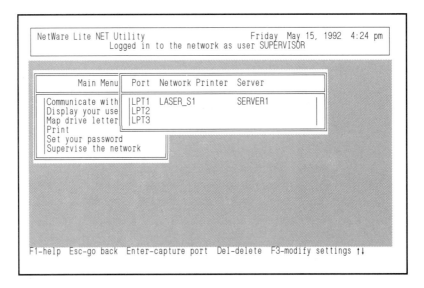

You will find additional information about the individual options of this window in Chapter 7.

5.   To accept the default settings and exit, press Esc.

After this window disappears from the screen, you return to the display of the available ports, where information about the assigned network printer is displayed:

```
NetWare Lite NET Utility                      Friday  May 15, 1992  4:24 pm
                   Logged in to the network as user SUPERVISOR


        ┌─────────────────┐┌─────────────────────────────────────┐
        │      Main Menu  ││ Port  Network Printer   Server       │
        │┌────────────────┴┴──────┐─────────────────────────────  │
        ││Communicate with ││LPT1  LASER_S1          SERVER1      │
        ││Display your use ││LPT2                                 │
        ││Map drive letter ││LPT3                                 │
        ││Print            │└─────────────────────────────────────┘
        ││Set your password│
        ││Supervise the network│
        └─────────────────┘




 F1-help  Esc-go back  Enter-capture port  Del-delete  F3-modify settings ↑↓
```

Display of the assigned network printers

6.   You can assign other network printers or exit NET by pressing Alt F10 and answering Yes at the exit prompt.

Assigning network printers

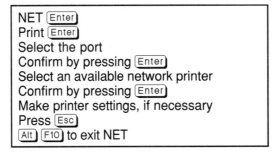

NET Enter
Print Enter
Select the port
Confirm by pressing Enter
Select an available network printer
Confirm by pressing Enter
Make printer settings, if necessary
Press Esc
Alt F10 to exit NET

4.4.2   Assigning network printers at DOS level

You can also assign network printers at DOS level without using NET.

In NetWare Lite you can use the NET CAPTURE command at the DOS level. For example, typing the following command at a workstation (client):

```
NET CAPTURE LPT1 LASER_S1 SERVER_1 Enter
```

takes all printer output for LPT1 on the workstation and sends it to the network printer named LASER_S1. The network printer was previously defined on the server named SERVER_1.

After the NET CAPTURE command, the following status report confirming the printer redirection is displayed:

```
Port LPT1 has been captured to NetWork Printer LASER_S1 on
server SERVER_S1.
```

You will find additional information about NET CAPTURE in Chapter 13 of this book.

4.4.3   Accessing a network printer

Now that you have defined and assigned a network printer, you probably want to know how to redirect printer output from the workstation (client) to the network printer.

Printing to a network printer is also called redirecting the printer output. The output from a workstation (client) is redirected to a defined, assigned network printer.

There are no other steps necessary for redirecting printer output. When you assign a network printer, NetWare Lite immediately begins handling output to the workstation (client) differently.

If you redirect the printer output of LPT1, then all output to this port is immediately redirected to the network printer assigned to this port. For example, you can print to LPT1 from your word processor and all output will be sent to the network printer assigned to LPT1.

4.4.4   Permanent assignment

Assignments for network printers are temporary. These are similar to assignments for network directories. When you assign a network printer to a workstation, it's only valid as long as you are logged in to the network.

We recommend placing the necessary specifications in a batch file that can be run to make the necessary printer assignments active.

The following is an example of such a batch file:

```
REM ******************************************************
REM PRINT.BAT From NetWare Lite Step by Step
REM Batch file for assigning network
REM printers to a workstation (client)
REM ******************************************************


REM ******************************************************
REM ASSIGNING NETWORK PRINTERS
REM ******************************************************
NET CAPTURE LPT1 LASER_S1 SERVER_1
NET CAPTURE LPT2 EPSON SERVER_2
NET CAPTURE LPT3 COLOR SERVER_6


REM ******************************************************
REM CLEAR SCREEN AND OUTPUT A MESSAGE
REM ******************************************************
@ CLS
@ ECHO   ******************************************************
@ ECHO   ********** ASSIGNMENT SUCCESSFUL ***************
@ ECHO   ******************************************************


REM ******************************************************
REM DISPLAY ASSIGNMENTS
REM ******************************************************
NET CAPTURE


REM **************************************** END OF FILE
```

This sample file contains three assignments for network printers, LASER_S1, EPSON and COLOR, which are all defined on different servers.

 You could combine the two batch files for mapping network directories and assigning network printers. By doing this, you could make all the necessary settings for a workstation by calling a single file.

With NetWare Lite Version 1.1, you can also use the NET SAVE command to automatically create a batch file, named NLLOGIN.BAT. This batch file, which will be placed in the root directory of drive C: (C:\), can be run to log you in to the network and set up the printer assignments and drive mappings. Use the NET SAVE command from the DOS prompt as follows:

```
NET SAVE [Enter]
```

The following message will be displayed to inform you that the settings were saved successfully:

```
Your network and environment settings were saved to
NLLOGIN.BAT.
```

You can now call the NLLOGIN.BAT file to automatically log in to the network and set up the network drives and assigned printers. After running STARTNET.BAT, use the following command to run NLLOGIN.BAT:

```
C:\NLLOGIN.BAT [Enter]
```

4.4.5 Displaying printer assignments

You can also use the NET CAPTURE command to display the current printer settings on the workstation.

This command displays the network printers assigned to the workstation (client), when used at the DOS prompt in the following manner:

```
NET CAPTURE [Enter]
```

you will see a list similar to the following:

```
                    currently Captured Local ports
Local port  Network printer  Server   Capture Settings
==========  ===============  ======   ================
LPT1        LASER_S1         SERVER1  Banner=Y Papertype=1 Hold=N
                                      Setup=DEFAULT
                                      Copies=1 Tabs=0  Formfeed=Y
                                      Direct=N Wait=10 Notify=N
```

This display informs you which network printers are assigned to the current workstation (client).

4.5 Verifying Network Connections

Problems connecting workstations to the existing network can be caused by a number of different things. For example, the cable connection could be damaged or one of the network cards might be defective.

To isolate the possible source of the error, NetWare Lite gives you an option for checking both the connection (cable) and the network cards. This option is part of the NetWare Lite installation program.

    You can use the following method to test the connections of the workstations and all the connections within a network, including the connections to the servers.

To test the hardware connection, perform the following steps:

1.   Start the workstation with the installed operating system.

2.   Next, load NetWare Lite, as described in the previous chapters (STARTNET.BAT).

    The Verify network connections option will not function unless the network drivers have been loaded.

3.   Insert the NetWare Lite diskette into drive A: (or a program diskette if you have 51/4" diskettes) and then change to this directory. Type the following from the DOS prompt:

        A: [Enter]

    If you are using drive B:, simply change the command (B: [Enter]).

4.   Then type the following to start the installation program:

        INSTALL [Enter]

After a short time, the main menu of the installation program appears on the screen, as shown in the following figure:

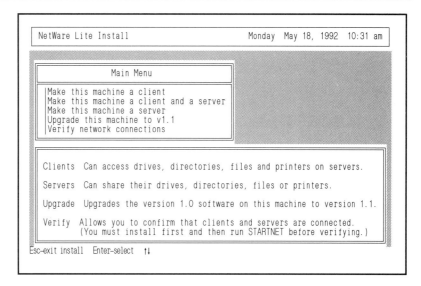

```
┌─────────────────────────────────────────────────────────────────────┐
│ NetWare Lite Install                    Monday  May 18, 1992  10:31 am │
│  ┌──────────────────────────────────────┐                             │
│  │              Main Menu               │                             │
│  │ Make this machine a client           │                             │
│  │ Make this machine a client and a server │                          │
│  │ Make this machine a server           │                             │
│  │ Upgrade this machine to v1.1         │                             │
│  │ Verify network connections           │                             │
│  └──────────────────────────────────────┘                             │
│  ┌────────────────────────────────────────────────────────────────┐   │
│  │ Clients  Can access drives, directories, files and printers on servers. │
│  │                                                                  │   │
│  │ Servers  Can share their drives, directories, files or printers. │   │
│  │                                                                  │   │
│  │ Upgrade  Upgrades the version 1.0 software on this machine to version 1.1. │
│  │                                                                  │   │
│  │ Verify   Allows you to confirm that clients and servers are connected. │
│  │          (You must install first and then run STARTNET before verifying.) │
│  └────────────────────────────────────────────────────────────────┘   │
│ Esc-exit install   Enter-select   ↑↓                                  │
└─────────────────────────────────────────────────────────────────────┘
```

The main menu of the installation program

5.   First, select *Verify network connections* by highlighting it with the cursor keys and pressing Enter.

A text box appears. Enter the name of the workstation you want to check.

   The name that you enter here doesn't have to be identical to a server name; it will only help identify the workstation. It's best if you use the term STATION, followed by a number or the user name. Make sure you give different names to different workstations.

6.   For example, type:

STATION_1

and then press Enter.

The name and address appear in an additional window on the screen. Each workstation in a network can be identified by the address.

7.   To verify the connection to another workstation within the network, follow the same steps at this workstation:

• Start operating system
• Load NetWare Lite

- Call the installation routine
- Select Verify network connections
- Enter a temporary name

After following these steps, if you find the same information on both screens, then the connection is in order.

For example, the following might appear on the screen:

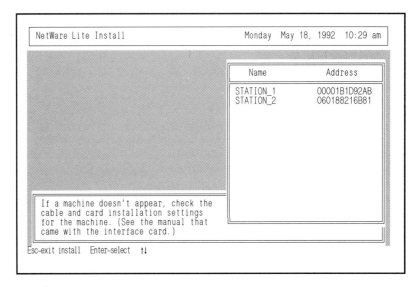

Display of tested stations

This display informs you that the hardware connection between the two workstations, STATION_1 and STATION_2) is working properly.

    If a station does not appear in the list, it indicates a hardware problem. This could be caused by a defective network card or a damaged cable connection.

8.   You can then test other workstations or exit the installation program by pressing [Esc] twice, and answering Yes to the Exit prompt.

Verifying connections

Necessary steps

```
Load NetWare Lite with STARTNET.BAT
Place NetWare Lite Diskette in drive A
A: [Enter]
INSTALL [Enter]
Select Verify network connections
Enter name for the workstation (temporary)
Confirm by pressing [Enter]
Test other workstations
Check connections on the screen
Press [Esc]
Answer security prompt with Yes
```

5. Managing Users

Before the users can log in to the network and begin to work, the system manager (SUPERVISOR) must do several things. First each user must be assigned a login name (user name), which enables the user to access the network.

The system manager (SUPERVISOR) is the only user that is allowed to create and delete user names. However, by using security equivalences other users can also be granted similar privileges.

The user name SUPERVISOR, which is intended for the system manager, will be created when NetWare Lite is installed. The login name SUPERVISOR cannot be deleted and its access privileges cannot be limited in any way. Since this login name is reserved for the system manager, it must have the power to modify all network parameters and the privileges of other login names.

NetWare Lite provides the NET utility to maintain user names. In addition to this, NET can also be used to define other parameters associated with user names. The following are some of the most important tasks this program can perform:

- Assigning access privileges
- Setting a password
- Setting the password expiration interval

5.1 Setting Up a New User

Use the following procedure to set up a new user on the NetWare Lite network.

1.   Start the NET utility from the DOS prompt with:

     NET [Enter]

     In this example, we assume that you have already logged into the network as the Supervisor (or an account with Supervisor privileges). As previously mentioned, only the network supervisor has the ability to add and delete user names. If you have not done so yet, you should exit NET by pressing the [Esc] key and login as Supervisor before continuing.

2. From the main menu, select the *Supervise the network* option using the cursor keys and press ⌊Enter⌋. A new menu of the options available to the network supervisor then appears, as shown in the next figure.

  If you need more information on using NetWare Lite menus, please refer to Chapter 3.

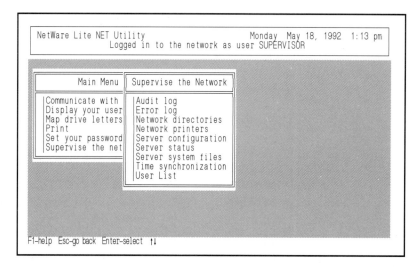

The NET main menu

3. Choose the *User List* option from the *Supervise the network* menu. This will display a list of all user names that have been defined on the network.

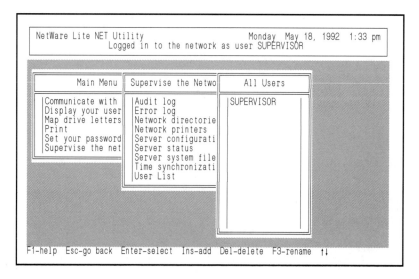

Display of user names

In this example only the user name supervisor has been defined on the network.

4.   Press ⌊Ins⌋ to add a new user name. A screen similar to the following will appear, allowing you to enter the new name.

    You can enter up to 15 characters for the user name. However, extremely long user names aren't practical because the complete user name must be entered with every login. Instead, you should use short, meaningful user names. You can enter a "full" user name later, which provides specific information about the user's identity.

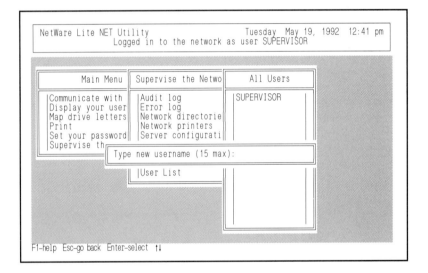

Entering a user name

5.   Enter the new user name and confirm your input by pressing ⌊Enter⌋.

6.   A screen will then appear that will allow you to set up specific account information for the new user. For example, you can define the users full name, network privileges and password requirements. The options are fully explained later:

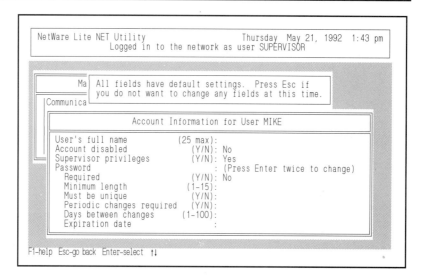

Defining the user account

User's full name

In addition to defining a user name, you can also assign a full name to a user. A full user name has a limit of 25 characters (in comparison to a 15 character limit on a user name), so more detailed information can be given to help identify a user.

Account disabled

The network supervisor can use this option to prevent a user from logging in to the network. If "Y" is entered at this prompt, the users account will be disabled and it will not be possible to access the network. Enter "N" at this prompt to re-enable access to the network.

Supervisor privileges

With NetWare Lite, all users are given supervisor privileges by default. If you would like to limit a users access to the NetWare Lite commands you should press "N" at this prompt to remove supervisor privileges.

Password

A password for the user can be entered or changed at this prompt. If a password is given, NetWare Lite will prompt the user for it when logging in. With out the correct password access to the network will be denied.

Required

To maintain greater security on the network, the network supervisor can require that passwords be used. This will help to prevent unauthorized users from gaining access to the network. If "Yes" is entered, the user will be required to log in using a password.

Minimum length

The network supervisor can also set the minimum length for a password. Since a longer password is harder to guess, this also helps secure the network. Valid lengths are between 1 and 15 characters.

Must be unique

If "Y" is entered, users will be unable to reuse an old password.

Periodic changes req.

This is used with the *Days between changes* option that follows. Entering "Yes" at this prompt will require users to change their password on a regular basis.

Days between changes

This is used with the *Periodic changes req.* prompt, to specify the number of days a user can use the same password. Valid options are between 1 and 100 days.

Expiration date

If the network supervisor requires that the password is changed, the date the current password expires will be displayed here. The user must change the password before this date.

7. You should make the necessary changes to the users account and press [Esc] to add the new user name, or simply press [Esc] to accept the default settings and add the new user name. The name will then be displayed in the list of current users.

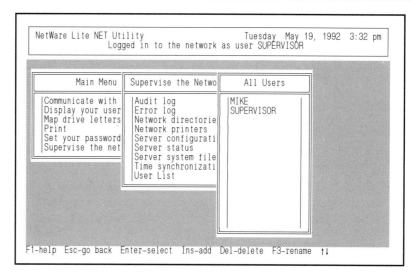

```
NetWare Lite NET Utility                    Tuesday  May 19, 1992  3:32 pm
                 Logged in to the network as user SUPERVISOR

         ┌──────────────┐┌──────────────────┐┌─────────────────┐
         │  Main Menu   ││Supervise the Netwo││    All Users    │
         ├──────────────┤├──────────────────┤├─────────────────┤
         │Communicate with││Audit log        ││MIKE             │
         │Display your user││Error log        ││SUPERVISOR       │
         │Map drive letters││Network directorie│                 │
         │Print         ││Network printers  ││                 │
         │Set your password││Server configurati│                 │
         │Supervise the net││Server status    ││                 │
         └──────────────┘│Server system file│                 │
                          │Time synchronizati│                 │
                          │User List         ││                 │
                          └──────────────────┘│                 │
                                               └─────────────────┘
    F1-help  Esc-go back  Enter-select  Ins-add  Del-delete  F3-rename  ↑↓
```

The list of current user names

Now you've successfully defined a new user name. You can repeat this procedure to add additional user names or exit NET by pressing Alt F10 and answering "Yes" to the *Exit NET* prompt that follows.

Adding a new user name

Necessary steps

```
NET Enter
Supervise the network Enter
User list Enter
Press Ins
Type the new user name and press Enter to confirm the input
Set account options and press Esc
Press Alt F10 and answer "Yes" to the exit prompt
```

5.2   Changing a User Name

The following steps are needed in order to change a user name that has already been created:

1.   Start NET from the DOS prompt with:

          NET Enter

2.   From the main menu, select the *Supervise the network* option using the cursor keys and press Enter. A new menu of the options available to the network supervisor then appears.

3. Select the *User list* option from the *Supervise the network* menu to display a list of the current network users.

4. Use the cursor keys to move the selection bar to the user name that you would like to change and press [F3].

5. The selected user name will appear in a separate input line. Use [Backspace] to remove the "old" name.

6. Type in the new user name and press the [Enter] key to confirm the input.

7. The new user name will then appear in the list of current users.

You have now completed the procedure for changing a user name with NET. You can continue within NET or exit by pressing [Alt] [F10] and then answering "Yes" to the *Exit NET* prompt that follows.

Changing a user name

Necessary steps

```
NET [Enter]
Supervise the network [Enter]
User list [Enter]
Select the user name to change
Press [F3]
Type in the new user name
Press [Enter] to confirm the input
Press [Alt] [F10] and answer "Yes" to the exit prompt
```

5.3   Deleting a User Name

NetWare Lite allows the Supervisor (or a user with supervisor privileges) to delete one or more user names. However, you must be very careful when using this privilege. Once a user name has been deleted, all information associated with it is permanently lost. If you accidentally delete a user name, you cannot restore it by simply re-entering the name. All of the parameters that were associated with the user name must be reset. If you're sure that you want to delete a particular user name, follow this procedure:

     You cannot delete the user name Supervisor or the user name you are currently logged in under.

1. Start NET from the DOS prompt with:

NET [Enter]

2.   From the main menu, select the *Supervise the network* option using the cursor keys and press [Enter]. A new menu of the options available to the network supervisor then appears.

3.   Select the *User list* option from the *Supervise the network* menu to display a list of the current network users.

4.   Use the cursor keys to move the selection bar to the user name that you would like to delete and press [Del].

☞   If you need to delete more than one user name, you can use the [F5] key to make multiple selections. Please see the section on using NetWare menus in Chapter 3 for additional information.

5.   A prompt, asking whether you want to delete this user name, will appear.

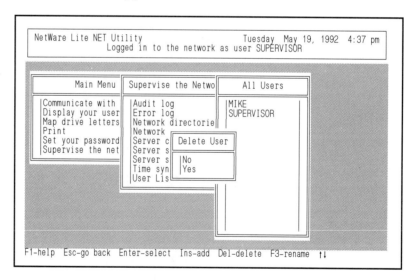

Deleting a user entry

6.   If you are sure you would like to delete the user name, press [Enter] to answer "Yes".

You have now completed the procedure for deleting a user name with NET. You can continue within NET or exit by pressing [Alt] [F10] and then answering "Yes" to the *Exit NET* prompt that follows.

Deleting a user name

Necessary steps

```
NET [Enter]
Supervise the network [Enter]
User list [Enter]
Select the user name to delete
Press [Del]
Answer "Yes" to the Delete User prompt and press [Enter]
Press [Alt] [F10] and answer "Yes" to the exit prompt
```

5.4 Assigning a Full User Name

In addition to defining a user name, as described in Section 4.1, you can also assign a full name to a user.

Full user names can help identify the users on the network. While user names are limited to 15 characters, and are best kept short to simplify logging in, full user names can be up to 25 characters long.

To assign a full user name to a user, use the following procedure:

1. Start NET from the DOS prompt with:

    NET [Enter]

2. From the main menu, select the *Supervise the network* option using the cursor keys and press [Enter]. A new menu of the options available to the network supervisor then appears.

3. Select the *User list* option from the *Supervise the network* menu to display a list of the user names that have been defined.

4. Use the cursor keys to select the user name for which you want to define a full user name and press [Enter]. A screen similar to the following will appear:

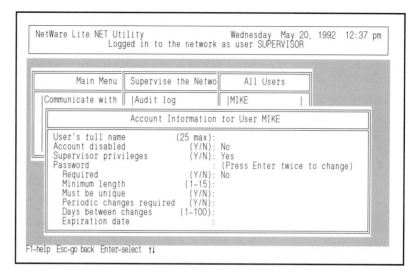

Assigning a full user name

5.   Press Enter to select *User's full name* and type in the desired
      name. When finished, press Enter to confirm the input.

      You can enter up to 25 characters for the full user name.

6.   Press Esc and answer "Yes" to the *Save changes* prompt to
      save the full user name.

Now you've assigned a full user name to the selected user name.
You can continue to work within NET or exit the program by
pressing Alt F10 and answering "Yes" to the prompt that follows.

Assigning a full user name

Necessary steps

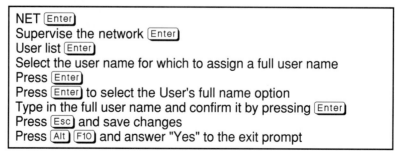

5.5   Changing or Deleting a Full User Name

If you want to change or delete the full user name, follow these steps:

1.   Start NET from the DOS prompt with:

     NET (Enter)

2.   From the main menu, select the *Supervise the network* option using the cursor keys and press (Enter). A new menu of the options available to the network supervisor then appears.

3.   Select the *User list* option from the *Supervise the network* menu to display a list of the user names that have been defined.

4.   Use the cursor keys to move the selection bar to the user name for which you want to change or delete the full user name and confirm your selection with (Enter).

5.   Press (Enter) again to select *User's full name.*

6.   You can then use the (Backspace) key to remove the old name. If you would like to delete the old name press (Enter). If you would like to change the name, type in the new name and press (Enter) to confirm the new full name. You should then answer "Yes" to save the changes.

     If you are changing the full user name, you can enter up to 25 characters.

7.   Press (Esc) and answer "Yes" to the *Save changes* prompt to save the full user name.

Now you've changed or deleted the full user name. You can continue to work within NET or exit the program by pressing (Alt) (F10) and answering "Yes" to the *Exit NET* prompt that follows.

Deleting a full user name

Necessary steps

```
NET [Enter]
Supervise the network [Enter]
User list [Enter]
Select the user name for which to delete the full user name
Press [Enter]
Press [Enter] to select the User's full name option
Use [Backspace] to remove the full user name
Press [Enter] to confirm the input
Press [Esc] and save changes
Press [Alt] [F10] and answer "Yes" to the exit prompt
```

Changing a full user name

Necessary steps

```
NET [Enter]
Supervise the network [Enter]
User list [Enter]
Select the user name for which to delete the full user name
Press [Enter]
Press [Enter] to select the User's full name option
Use [Backspace] to remove the full user name
Type in the new full user name
Press [Enter] to confirm the input
Press [Esc] and save changes
Press [Alt] [F10] and answer "Yes" to the exit prompt
```

5.6   Granting Supervisor Privileges

As Supervisor, you can grant individual users supervisor privileges. This allows a user to perform certain functions that are usually only allowed for the Supervisor, for example, adding new users. The following is the procedure for granting supervisor privileges to a user:

   With NetWare Lite, all users are given supervisor privileges by default. It's only necessary to grant a user supervisor privileges if they have been previously revoked.

1.   Start NET from the DOS prompt with:

        NET [Enter]

2. From the main menu, select the *Supervise the network* option using the cursor keys and press (Enter). A new menu of the options available to the network supervisor then appears.

3. Select the *User list* option from the *Supervise the network* menu to display a list of the user names that have been defined.

4. Use the cursor keys to move the selection bar to the user name for which you want to grant supervisor privileges and confirm your selection with (Enter).

5. Select the *Supervisor privileges* item, using the cursor keys, and press (Y) to select "Yes".

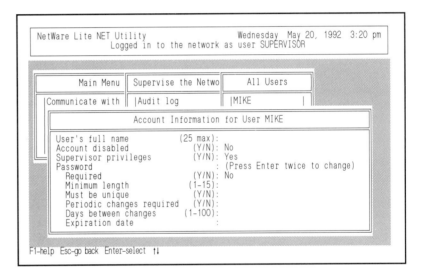

Granting supervisor privileges

6. Confirm the change in the *Supervisor privileges* field by pressing (Enter).

7. Press (Esc) and answer "Yes" to the *Save changes* prompt to save the new setting.

That completes the process of granting supervisor privileges to the user. You can continue to work within NET or exit the program by pressing (Alt) (F10) and answering "Yes" to the *Exit NET* prompt that follows.

Granting supervisor privileges

Necessary steps

NET [Enter]
Supervise the network [Enter]
User list [Enter]
Select the user name for which to grant supervisor privileges
Press [Enter]
Select the Supervisor privileges item
Press [N] to grant supervisor privileges
Press [Enter] to confirm the input
Press [Esc] and save changes
Press [Alt] [F10] and answer "Yes" to the exit prompt

5.7   Revoking Supervisor Privileges

It's also possible to revoke supervisor privileges from a user. If you would like to limit a users access to the network resources, you must revoke that users supervisor privileges. Follow these steps:

With NetWare Lite, all users are given supervisor privileges by default. You must revoke a users supervisor privileges to control access to the network.

1.   Start NET from the DOS prompt with:

      NET [Enter]

2.   From the main menu, select the *Supervise the network* option using the cursor keys and press [Enter]. A new menu of the options available to the network supervisor then appears.

3.   Select the *User list* option from the *Supervise the network* menu to display a list of the user names that have been defined.

4.   Use the cursor keys to move the selection bar to the user name for which you want to revoke supervisor privileges and confirm your selection with [Enter].

5.   Select the *Supervisor privileges* item, using the cursor keys, and press [N] to select "No".

6.   Confirm the change in the *Supervisor privileges* field by pressing [Enter].

7.   Press (Esc) and answer "Yes" to the *Save changes* prompt to save the new setting.

That completes the process of revoking a users supervisor privileges. You can continue to work within NET or exit the program by pressing (Alt) (F10) and answering "Yes" to the *Exit NET* prompt that follows.

Revoking supervisor privileges

Necessary steps

NET (Enter)
Supervise the network (Enter)
User list (Enter)
Select the user name for which to revoke supervisor privileges
Press (Enter)
Select the Supervisor privileges item
Press (N) to revoke supervisor privileges
Press (Enter) to confirm the input
Press (Esc) and save changes
Press (Alt) (F10) and answer "Yes" to the exit prompt

5.8   Assigning a Password to a User

A primary concern of the network supervisors is to keep unauthorized users from gaining access to the network data. To help with this, NetWare Lite allows the use of passwords. The supervisor can assign a password to each user that must be entered before a user can access the network. Without the correct password, access to the network is denied. Use the following procedure to assign a password to a user:

1.   Start NET from the DOS prompt with:

      NET (Enter)

2.   From the main menu, select the *Supervise the network* option using the cursor keys and press (Enter). A new menu of the options available to the network supervisor then appears.

3.   Select the *User list* option from the *Supervise the network* menu to display a list of the user names that have been defined.

4.   Use the cursor keys to move the selection bar to the user name for which you want to assign a password and confirm your selection with [Enter].

5.   Use the cursor keys to select the *Password* item and press [Enter] twice.

6.   An input line will appear allowing you to type in the new password. Carefully type in the password and press [Enter] to confirm the input. You can use any combination of up to 15 characters.

   When you type in a password remember that passwords are never displayed on the screen. This ensures that no other user can gain access to your password by watching you type it in.

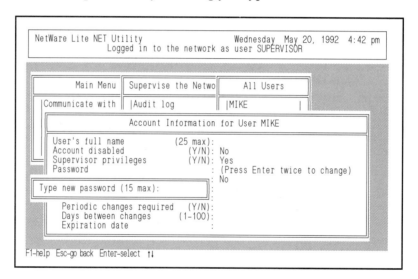

```
 NetWare Lite NET Utility                   Wednesday  May 20, 1992  4:42 pm
                     Logged in to the network as user SUPERVISOR

        ┌───────────────┬──────────────────┬──────────────────┐
        │   Main Menu    ║ Supervise the Netwo║   All Users      │
        ├───────────────╢                  ╟──────────────────┤
        │Communicate with║ │Audit log        ║ │MIKE            │
        ├───────────────────────────────────────────────┐
        │       Account Information for User MIKE         │
        ├───────────────────────────────────────────────┤
        │ User's full name        (25 max):              │
        │ Account disabled        (Y/N): No              │
        │ Supervisor privileges   (Y/N): Yes             │
        │ Password                     : (Press Enter twice to change)
        ┌───────────────────────────────┐  : No          │
        │ Type new password (15 max):   │  :             │
        └───────────────────────────────┘  :             │
        │   Periodic changes required  (Y/N):            │
        │   Days between changes    (1-100):             │
        │   Expiration date              :               │
        └───────────────────────────────────────────────┘

 F1-help  Esc-go back  Enter-select  ↑↓
```

Entering a password

7.   Type in the password and press [Enter] to confirm the input.

8.   Another input line will appear asking you to retype the password. Since you can't see the password when you type it in, this ensures that no typing errors were made. After retyping the password press [Enter] to confirm the input.

9.   Press [Esc] and answer "Yes" to the *Save changes* prompt to save the new setting.

The user will then be required to enter this password when logging in to the network. You can continue to work within NET or exit the program by pressing [Alt] [F10] and answering "Yes" to the *Exit NET* prompt that follows.

Assigning a password to a user

Necessary steps

```
NET [Enter]
Supervise the network [Enter]
User list [Enter]
Select the user name for which to assign a password
Press [Enter]
Select the password item
Press [Enter] twice
Type in the password and press [Enter]
Retype the password and press [Enter]
Press [Esc] and save changes
Press [Alt] [F10] and answer "Yes" to the exit prompt
```

5.9 Changing an Existing Password

If you need to change a user's password, you can follow the same steps that you used when assigning it. The necessary steps are listed below:

Only the network supervisor, or a user with supervisor privileges, can change another user's password. If you do not have supervisor privileges and would like to change your password, please see Section 5.10.

1.   Start NET from the DOS prompt with:

        NET [Enter]

2.   From the main menu, select the *Supervise the network* option using the cursor keys and press [Enter]. A new menu of the options available to the network supervisor then appears.

3.   Select the *User list* option from the *Supervise the network* menu to display a list of the user names that have been defined.

4.   Use the cursor keys to move the selection bar to the user name for which you want to change the password and confirm your selection with [Enter].

5.   Use the cursor keys to select the *Password* item and press
        Enter twice.

6.   An input line will appear allowing you to type in the new
        password. Carefully type in the password and press Enter to
        confirm the input. You can use any combination of up to 15
        characters.

        When you type in a password remember that
        passwords are never displayed on the screen. This
        ensures that no other user can gain access to your
        password by watching you type it in.

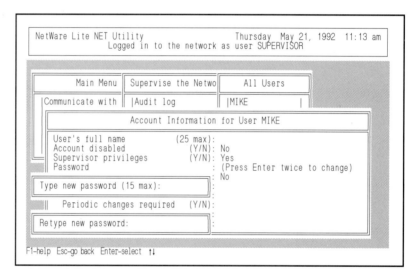

Entering a password

7.   Type in the password and press Enter to confirm the input.

8.   Another input line will appear asking you to retype the
        password. Since you can't see the password when you type it
        in, this ensures that no typing errors were made. After
        retyping the password press Enter to confirm the input.

9.   Press Esc and answer "Yes" to the *Save changes* prompt to
        save the new setting.

The user will then be required to enter this password when logging
in to the network. You can continue to work within NET or exit the
program by pressing Alt F10 and answering "Yes" to the *Exit NET*
prompt that follows.

Changing an existing password

Necessary steps

```
NET (Enter)
Supervise the network (Enter)
User list (Enter)
Select the user name for which to change the password
Press (Enter)
Select the password item
Press (Enter) twice
Type in the password and press (Enter)
Retype the password and press (Enter)
Press (Esc) and save changes
Press (Alt) (F10) and answer "Yes" to the exit prompt
```

5.10   Changing your Personal User Password

If you need to change your password, it can easily be done from the NET *Main Menu*. Use the following steps to change your personal user password:

1.   Start NET from the DOS prompt with:

        NET (Enter)

2.   From the main menu, select the *Set your password* option using the cursor keys and press (Enter).

3.   If a password had been previously defined, you will be asked to enter the old password first. You should enter your old password and press (Enter).

4.   After confirming the old password, or if a password was never assigned, an input line will appear that allows you to type in a maximum of 15 characters for the new password. Enter the new password and press (Enter).

    When you type in a password remember that passwords are never displayed on the screen. This ensures that no other user can gain access to your password by watching you type it in.

5.   Another input line will appear asking you to retype the password. Since you can't see the password when you type it in, this ensures that no typing errors were made. After retyping the password press (Enter) to confirm the input.

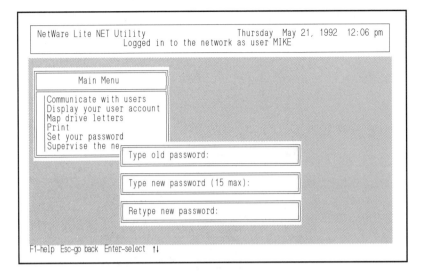

```
NetWare Lite NET Utility                Thursday  May 21, 1992  12:06 pm
                 Logged in to the network as user MIKE
```

Entering a password

6. The password setting will be saved and you will be returned to the *Main Menu*.

You will then be required to enter the new password the next time you log in to the network. You can continue to work within NET or exit the program by pressing [Alt] [F10] and answering "Yes" to the *Exit NET* prompt that follows.

Changing your personal user password

Necessary steps

NET [Enter]
Set your password [Enter]
Type in your old password, if necessary, and press [Enter]
Type in the new password and press [Enter]
Retype the new password and press [Enter]
Press [Alt] [F10] and answer "Yes" to the exit prompt

5.11   Other Password Options

There are several other password options that the network supervisor can use to maintain network security. For example, the supervisor can require that the network users use a password when logging in to the network and that the password is changed on a regular basis.

We'll describe each of these options later. You may make any changes that your system requires simply by selecting the option from the *Account information* screen and making the appropriate entry.

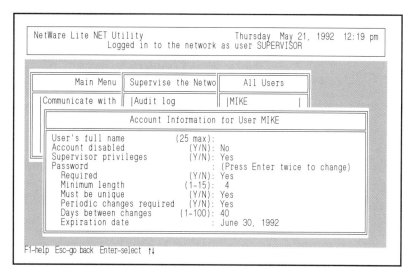

Setting the other password options

  If you use these options to limit users access to the network, be sure that you also revoke the user's supervisor privileges. If a user has supervisor privileges, that user can change any password settings that have been made.

Required

This option allows the supervisor to require that the user use a password. If this is set to "Yes" the user must use a password to log in to the network. If *Required* is set to "No" the user may or may not use a password.

Minimum length

Since longer passwords are harder to guess, this option allows the supervisor to define the minimum length of the user's password. If the user changes his/her password, it must contain no less than the number of characters specified at this prompt.

Must be unique

Setting this prompt to "Yes" will force users to use a new password each time it's changed. This prevents users from re-using an old password.

Periodic changes required

The supervisor can also require that users change their password on a regular basis. If a user's password is never changed, there is a greater chance that someone else will figure it out. This option is used with the *Days between changes* option that follows.

Days between changes

If you have required that a user make periodic changes to his/her password, you can specify the number of days between changes. You can enter a number of days between 1 and 100. After that period of time expires, the user must change the password to maintain access to the network.

Expiration date

If you have required that the user make periodic changes to the password, this will display the date that the password expires.

5.12   Disabling a Users Account

If you must disable a user's account temporarily, it can be done easily from within NET. This will prevent a user from logging in, until you re-enable the access to the network, as described in Section 5.13.

   If you would like to permanently remove a user's access to the network, you can delete the user name as described in Section 5.3.

1.   Start NET from the DOS prompt with:

       NET (Enter)

2.   From the main menu, select the *Supervise the network* option using the cursor keys and press (Enter). A new menu of the options available to the network supervisor then appears.

3.   Select the *User list* option from the *Supervise the network* menu to display a list of the user names that have been defined.

4.   Use the cursor keys to move the selection bar to the user name for which you want to revoke access and confirm your selection with (Enter).

5. Select the *Account disabled* item, using the cursor keys, and press Ⓨ to select "Yes".

6. Confirm the change in the *Account disabled* field by pressing Enter.

7. Press Esc and answer "Yes" to the *Save changes* prompt to save the new setting.

 Remember that the user will have no access to the network or network resources until you re-enable the account.

That completes the process of disabling a users access to the network. You can continue to work within NET or exit the program by pressing Alt F10 and answering "Yes" to the *Exit NET* prompt that follows.

Disabling a user's account

Necessary steps

```
NET Enter
Supervise the network Enter
User list Enter
Select the user name for which to revoke access
Press Enter
Select the Account disabled item
Press Ⓨ to disable the user's account
Press Enter to confirm the input
Press Esc and save changes
Press Alt F10 and answer "Yes" to the exit prompt
```

5.13 Re-enabling a Users Account

If you have disabled a user's account, you must re-enable it before that user will have any access to the network resources. Please use the following procedure to re-enable a user's account.

1. Start NET from the DOS prompt with:

   NET Enter

2. From the main menu, select the *Supervise the network* option using the cursor keys and press Enter. A new menu of the options available to the network supervisor then appears.

3.   Select the *User list* option from the *Supervise the network* menu to display a list of the user names that have been defined.

4.   Use the cursor keys to move the selection bar to the user name for which you want to grant access to the network and confirm your selection with [Enter].

5.   Select the *Account disabled* item, using the cursor keys, and press [N] to select "No".

6.   Confirm the change in the *Account disabled* field by pressing [Enter].

7.   Press [Esc] and answer "Yes" to the *Save changes* prompt to save the new setting.

That completes the process of re-enabling a user's access to the network. You can continue to work within NET or exit the program by pressing [Alt] [F10] and answering "Yes" to the *Exit NET* prompt that follows.

Re-enabling a user's account

Necessary steps

```
NET [Enter]
Supervise the network [Enter]
User list [Enter]
Select the user name for which to re-enable access
Press [Enter]
Select the Account disabled item
Press [N] to re-enable the user's account
Press [Enter] to confirm the input
Press [Esc] and save changes
Press [Alt] [F10] and answer "Yes" to the exit prompt
```

6.   Access Rights Under NetWare Lite

Defining access rights is another important factor in setting up new usernames. Without the necessary rights, it's impossible for users to take advantage of the diverse options of a network. For example, users cannot access files and/or programs within the system until they have been granted access rights.

     The only user who doesn't need to be assigned special rights is the supervisor. The supervisor is granted all the access rights when the network is installed. It's also impossible to revoke or limit the supervisor's access rights.

The information about access rights in this chapter has to do with the rights to use network directories. Access rights for using network printers are discussed in the next chapter.

There are two different procedures for assigning access rights in NetWare Lite. You can grant default access rights to a network directory (for all users) or you can assign each user individual access rights, called nondefault rights.

     The default access rights will apply to all users. If an individual user requires different access rights, nondefault access rights must be given to that user.

Access rights under NetWare Lite

The term "access right" is commonly used with NetWare Lite and other network operating systems.

Access rights are used to define the kinds of access the individual users, within the network, have to the files stored in a network directory. For example, the supervisor can determine that users may read certain files, but never make changes to them. In other words, the users have read access but not write access.

NetWare Lite provides you with the following access rights when you setup network directories:

ALL

Allows unrestricted access to the files of the specified directory. Users may read, delete, execute and make changes to files. This is the highest priority level of access rights for network directories.

NONE

No access of any kind is permitted.

READ

Users may read files, but may not make changes to, or delete files. NetWare Lite comes supplied with the NET utility program for assigning and defining access rights. This program will be used throughout the following sections.

6.1   Assigning Default Access Rights

Although setting up a username is one of the most important requirements for a user to work in a network, assigning access rights for the network directory is almost as important.

For example, a user must be granted the right to execute programs, read files or make changes to them if they are stored in a network directory. The following steps will enable you to define or modify the default access rights of a network directory:

1.   First call the NET utility program, using the following command:

        NET [Enter]

2.   Then select *Supervise the network* option in the main menu of NET and press [Enter].

     If you are not familiar with the operation of the NetWare Lite menus, read Chapter 3 of this book. You will find detailed information about operating this menu there.

        You can also call online help at any time by pressing [F1].

3.   Select the *Network directories* item from the *Supervise the network* menu. A list of the defined network directories appears, as shown in the following figure:

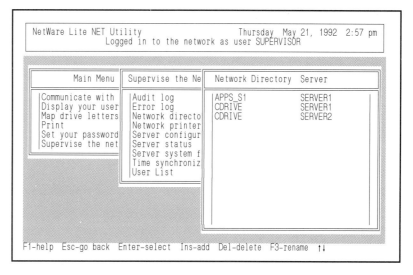

```
┌──────────────────────────────────────────────────────────────────────┐
│ NetWare Lite NET Utility                    Thursday  May 21, 1992  2:57 pm │
│              Logged in to the network as user SUPERVISOR              │
│ ┌────────────────────────────────────────────────────────────────┐ │
│ │┌──────────────┬─────────────────┬─────────────────────────────┐ │ │
│ ││   Main Menu   │ Supervise the Ne│ Network Directory   Server  │ │ │
│ │├──────────────┼─────────────────┼─────────────────────────────┤ │ │
│ ││Communicate with││Audit log        │APPS_S1          SERVER1     │ │ │
│ ││Display your user││Error log        │CDRIVE           SERVER1     │ │ │
│ ││Map drive letters││Network directo  │CDRIVE           SERVER2     │ │ │
│ ││Print          ││Network printer  │                             │ │ │
│ ││Set your password││Server configur  │                             │ │ │
│ ││Supervise the net││Server status    │                             │ │ │
│ ││               ││Server system f  │                             │ │ │
│ ││               ││Time synchroniz  │                             │ │ │
│ ││               ││User List        │                             │ │ │
│ │└──────────────┘└───────────────┘                             │ │ │
│ │                                 └─────────────────────────────┘ │ │
│ └────────────────────────────────────────────────────────────────┘ │
│ F1-help  Esc-go back  Enter-select  Ins-add  Del-delete  F3-rename ↑↓ │
└──────────────────────────────────────────────────────────────────────┘
```

Display of the available network directories

 You can read about setting up network directories in Chapter 3 of this book.

When you install a network directory for the first time, NetWare Lite automatically assigns it ALL access rights.

4. Use the cursor keys to select the name of the network directory whose default access rights you want to change.

 During installation, NetWare Lite automatically assigns the name CDRIVE. This name refers to the root directory of the hard drive of the server. This enables access to the entire hard drive, including subdirectories.

This is a default setting. However, we recommend deleting this default setting. If this is not changed, every user will have access to the entire hard drive.

To delete this name, simply move the selection bar to it (CDRIVE) and then press Del. After you confirm the security prompt by answering Yes, the name is removed from the list.

5. After you confirm your choice of network directory by pressing Enter, a window appears with additional information on the selected directory:

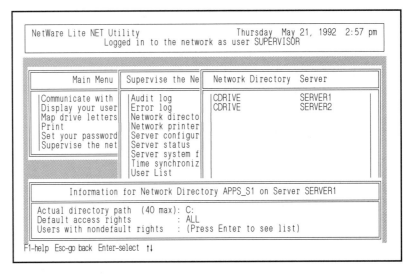

Additional information about the selected network directory

6.   In the *Default access rights* text box you will find the specification of default access rights. To change this setting, use the cursor keys to select this item and press Enter.

A new window appears showing the access right options that are available:

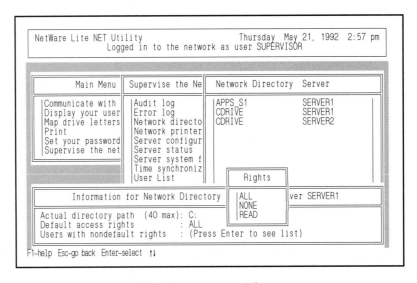

Selecting access rights

7.   Now select the option you want to assign as the default access right to the selected directory. Use the cursor keys to select it and press Enter.

The next section tells you how to change the access rights of individual users.

8.   The access right you selected then appears in the window after *Default access rights*.

9.   You can exit this window and return to the list of network directories by pressing (Esc).

10.   You can either continue working within NET or exit by pressing (Alt) (F10) and answering "Yes" to the *Exit NET* prompt.

You have just assigned default access rights for a directory. In the next section, you will learn how to assign nondefault access rights for individual users.

Assigning Default access rights

Necessary steps

```
NET (Enter)
Supervise the network (Enter)
Network directories (Enter)
Select the desired network directory
Confirm by pressing (Enter)
Select Default access rights and press (Enter)
Select desired access rights from the list
Confirm by pressing (Enter)
Press (Esc)
Press (Alt) (F10)  to exit
Answer Exit prompt with "Yes"
```

6.2   Assigning Nondefault Access Rights

Now that you have assigned general access rights to a network directory, we'll explain how to "customize" those rights for individual users. Let's suppose that you assigned READ to a network directory as a default access right. That means that all users can only read the files in this directory; none of the users will be able to edit the files.

However, if you want to grant a certain user the right to make changes to the existing files, NetWare Lite has a solution. This solution consists of assigning individual users rights that differ from the default access rights for the network directory or nondefault access rights.

Here are the steps for assigning a user nondefault access rights to a network directory:

1.   First call the NET utility program, using the following command:

      NET [Enter]

2.   Then select *Supervise the network* option in the main menu of NET.

3.   Select the *Network directories* item from the *Supervise the network* menu to display a list of the defined network directories.

4.   Use the cursor keys to select the network directory for which you want to assign nondefault access rights.

5.   Confirm your selection by pressing [Enter]. Another window appears, with information about the selected network directory.

6.   Select the *Users with nondefault rights* option in the window showing the network directory information.

7.   Now press [Enter] to see a list of users who already have nondefault rights for this network directory. If no one has been assigned nondefault rights for this network directory, the list will be empty.

8.   Next, press [Ins] to see a list of defined usernames.

9.   Select the user whom you want to assign nondefault access rights.

10.   After you confirm your selection by pressing [Enter], another window appears, displaying the possible access rights.

11.   Select the access right you want to assign to the user as nondefault right for the network directory.

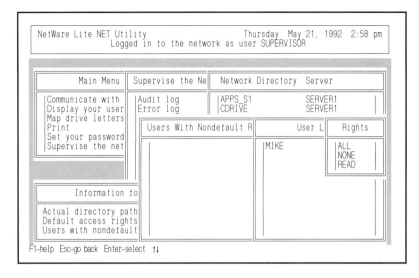

Selecting access rights

12.   After you press ⌈Enter⌉, the selected username and assigned access right appear on the screen, as shown in the next figure:

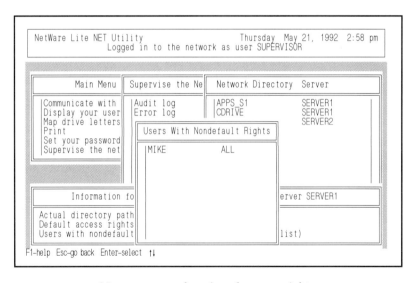

User name and assigned access right

   To assign nondefault access rights to other users for the selected directory, simply press ⌈Ins⌉ again and follow the same procedure.

13.   To exit the list of usernames with nondefault rights, press ⌈Esc⌉.

Remember that if you exit NET here by pressing [Alt]
[F10], all the changes you made will be lost.

14.   To save the settings, you must press [Esc] again, which
       returns you to the list of available network directories.

15.   Now you can make further settings or exit NET safely by
       pressing [Alt] [F10] and answering "Yes" to the *Exit NET*
       prompt.

You should now be familiar with the steps necessary for assigning
nondefault access rights for a network directory. The new access
rights you assigned will be valid the next time the user logs in to
the network.

Assigning nondefault access rights

Necessary steps

```
NET [Enter]
Supervise the network [Enter]
Network directories [Enter]
Move highlight to desired network directory
Confirm by pressing [Enter]
Users with nondefault rights [Enter]
Press [Ins] and select a username
Confirm by pressing [Enter]
Select desired access rights
Confirm by pressing [Enter]
Press [Esc] twice
Press [Alt] [F10] to exit
Answer Exit NET prompt with "Yes"
```

6.3   Changing Nondefault Access Rights

From time to time you will probably need to change the nondefault
access rights of a user (*Users with nondefault rights*) for a certain
network directory.

In this case, use the following steps to make the desired change:

1.   Call the NET utility program and select *Supervise the
      network* in the main menu.

2.   To display a list of defined network directories, select
      Network directories from the *Supervise the network*
      submenu.

3.   Select the network directory for which you want to change
      the nondefault access rights. An additional window appears
      with more information on the selected network directory.

4.   Use the cursor keys to select *Users with nondefault rights*
      and confirm your selection by pressing (Enter). This will
      display a list of users who have been assigned nondefault
      access rights for this network directory.

5.   Select the username whose access rights you want to change.

6.   After confirming your selection with (Enter), a screen similar
      to the following will appear.

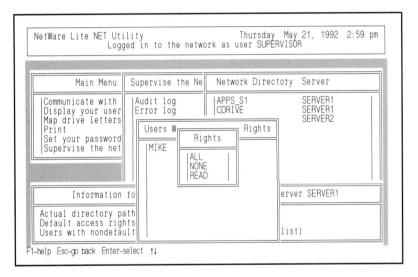

Selecting access rights

7.   Three possible access rights are displayed here. Select the
      desired option and press (Enter).

8.   The list of usernames and their access rights will be
      displayed again.

☞   If you exit NET here by pressing (Alt) (F10), all the
      changes you made will be lost.

9.   Press (Esc) twice to save the changes you made and exit.

10.   This returns you to the list of available network directories.
      You can make further changes here or exit the NET program
      by pressing (Alt) (F10) and answering "Yes" the *Exit NET*
      prompt.

You can use these steps to change the assigned nondefault access rights of a user at any time. The settings are automatically valid the next time the user logs in, and when you assign nondefault access rights to a user for the first time.

Changing nondefault access rights

Necessary steps

```
NET (Enter)
Supervise the network (Enter)
Network directories (Enter)
Select the desired network directory
Confirm by pressing (Enter)
Users with nondefault rights (Enter)
Select desired username
Confirm by pressing (Enter)
Select desired access rights
Confirm by pressing (Enter)
Press (Esc) twice
Press (Alt) (F10) to exit
Answer Exit NET prompt with "Yes"
```

6.4   Information About Nondefault Access Rights

When you work in a directory, it's important to be able to find out about your assigned access rights at any time. NetWare Lite provides you with a command for calling the desired information at the DOS prompt.

After logging in, simply type the following command:

```
NET NDLIST (Enter)
```

You will then see a list on the screen similar to the following:

```
Network Directory    Server         Your Rights
===================  ==========     ============

CDRIVE               SERVER1        READ
DATABASE_S1          SERVER1        NONE
APPS_S1              SERVER1        ALL

Total Network Directories:  3
```

You will be given a list of the available network directories and also information about the nondefault access rights. These are the rights assigned to you by the supervisor for accessing the network directory.

6.5   Removing Default Access Rights to a Directory

When you want to perform certain tasks in a network directory, such as install new programs or make settings to programs, you should make sure that no other user can access the directory during this time.

To temporarily suppress access to a network directory, you can use the principle of default access rights. Simply assign NONE as a default access right to the network directory.

In place of temporarily "locking" a file directory, you could also delete the network directory from the list of available network directories. However, this is more trouble than it's worth, because then you would have to re-install the network directory after making the changes.

To temporarily suppress access to a network directory, follow the next steps:

1.   After calling NET, select *Supervise the network*.

2.   Next, select *Network directories* from the *Supervise the network* menu to display a list of the defined network directories.

3.   Select the name of the network directory for which you want to temporarily remove the default access rights.

4.   Press (Enter) to confirm your selection. A window displaying information about the selected network directory will appear.

5.   Then select Default access rights. The default access rights currently assigned to the network directory will appear.

   ☞   You should see either ALL or READ here. If the entry reads NONE, then the default access rights for this network directory have already been removed. In such a case, press (Esc) to exit this window.

6.   To assign the access right NONE to the selected directory, press (Enter) to display the list of the possible access rights.

7.   Select the NONE option and confirm your selection by pressing (Enter).

The new assignment will then appear in the window displaying the directory information, as shown in the following figure:

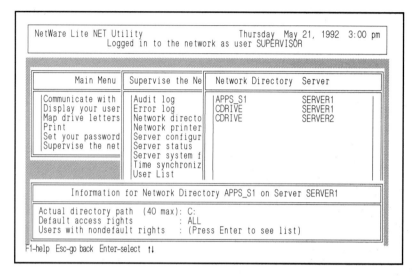

```
NetWare Lite NET Utility                      Thursday  May 21, 1992  3:00 pm
                     Logged in to the network as user SUPERVISOR

        Main Menu    | Supervise the Ne | Network Directory   Server
    Communicate with | Audit log        | APPS_S1              SERVER1
    Display your user| Error log        | CDRIVE               SERVER1
    Map drive letters| Network directo  | CDRIVE               SERVER2
    Print            | Network printer  |
    Set your password| Server configur  |
    Supervise the net| Server status    |
                     | Server system f  |
                     | Time synchroniz  |
                     | User List        |

          Information for Network Directory APPS_S1 on Server SERVER1

    Actual directory path  (40 max): C:
    Default access rights           : ALL
    Users with nondefault rights    : (Press Enter to see list)

 F1-help  Esc-go back  Enter-select  ↑↓
```

Display of information on a network directory

Remember that if you exit NET by pressing [Alt] [F10], all the changes you made will be lost.

8.   To be sure that the settings are saved, press [Esc] to return to the list of available network directories.

9.   Now you can make further changes or exit NET by pressing [Alt] [F10] and answering "Yes" to the *Exit NET* prompt.

You have just temporarily suppressed access to the selected network directory for all users on the network. Remember to change things back the way they were after you are finished making changes by assigning the same default access right to the network directory.

Removing default access rights

Necessary steps

```
NET Enter
Supervise the network Enter
Network directories Enter
Select the desired network directory
Confirm by pressing Enter
Default access rights Enter
Select access right NONE
Confirm by pressing Enter
Press Esc
Press Alt F10 to exit
Answer Exit NET prompt with "Yes"
```

6.6 Removing All Access Rights

The quickest way to prevent a single user from accessing a certain network directory is to remove all of his/her access rights to this directory. In other words, you assign the user the access right NONE. The following steps are necessary for this:

1.   First, load the NET utility program.

2.   Select *Supervise the network* from the main menu of this program.

3.   Select the menu item called *Network directories* from the submenu that appears. This causes a list of defined network directories to be displayed on the screen.

4.   Now select the name of the network directory you want to prevent the user from accessing.

5.   Press Enter to confirm your selection. An additional window appears with information about the selected network directory.

6.   In this additional window, select the *Users with nondefault rights* option.

7.   After confirming your selection by pressing Enter, you see a list of those users who have been assigned nondefault access rights for the selected network directory.

     If nondefault access rights haven't been assigned for the network directory yet, the list will be empty.

If you find the name of the user whose access rights you want to remove, select this username and press ⟨Enter⟩. Then continue with step 10.

8.   If the username is not contained in this list yet, press ⟨Ins⟩ to display a list of all usernames known to the network:

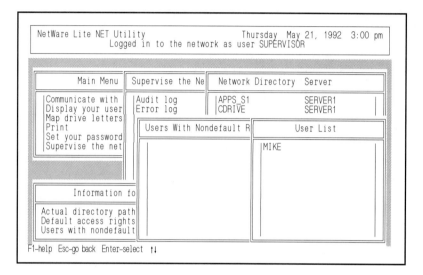

Display of available usernames

9.   Use the cursor keys to select the name of the user from this list.

10.   After pressing ⟨Enter⟩ to confirm your selection, another window appears, in which the nondefault access rights are displayed.

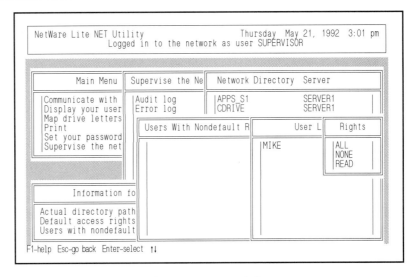

Selecting access rights

11.   Now select the access right NONE in this window and confirm it by pressing Enter.

12.   The selected username then appears on the screen with the assigned access right, as shown in the following figure.

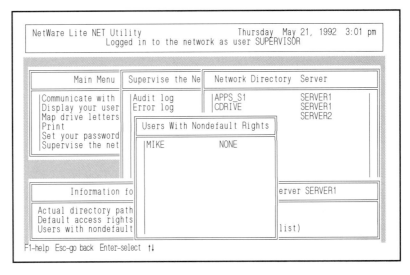

Username and assigned access right

To deny access to other users for the selected network directory, just press Ins again and follow the same steps.

13.   To exit the list of usernames (with nondefault access rights), press Esc.

Do not press [Alt] [F10] to exit NET until you have returned to the *Network directory* window. If you do, all the changes you made will be lost.

14.   After returning to the window showing the network directory information, press [Esc] again. This takes you back to the list of available network directories.

15.   Once here, you can make other settings or exit NET by pressing [Alt] [F10] and answering the exit prompt with Yes.

You have denied the user access to the selected network directory. This setting goes into effect the next time the user logs in. If the user attempts to access the network directory, an error message, stating that he/she no longer has any access rights in this directory, appears.

Removing all access rights

Necessary steps

```
NET [Enter]
Supervise the network [Enter]
Network directories [Enter]
Select the desired network directory
Confirm by pressing [Enter]
Select Users with nondefault rights [Enter]
Select desired Username
Confirm by pressing [Enter]
Select the access right NONE
Confirm by pressing [Enter]
Press [Esc] twice
Press [Alt] [F10] to exit
Answer exit prompt with "Yes"
```

7.   Printing In The NetWare Lite Network

One of the greatest advantages of using a network is that it allows you to share resources, such as printers. NetWare Lite also allows you to define network printers that can be shared by all users. Such a network printer can be connected to any server. The only requirement for user access is that the printer be defined as a network printer.

     Read Chapter 3 to learn how to set up network printers. Also remember that a network printer being set up for the first time is automatically assigned the ALL access right.

In the network, users select the command for printing whenever they like (i.e., they don't need to worry whether any other users are also sending print jobs at the same time); NetWare Lite is in charge of organizing all print jobs.

NetWare Lite collects print jobs in a *queue* and sends them to the printer one after the other. The print jobs are printed in accordance with the FIFO principle (First In First Out), so the jobs will be printed in the order in which they were placed in the queue.

You can display the contents of such a queue any time in NetWare Lite. You can delete print jobs from this display or define the number of copies that will be printed. You will learn how to do this and the principles involved as you read this chapter.

The difference between local printers and network printers

When you connect a printer to a stand-alone computer and address it from an application program or from the DOS prompt, you usually don't need to worry about how the print job is handled. The operating system is in charge of organizing this.

However, it's a different story when you use NetWare Lite. The operating system needs some additional information about how to process the incoming print jobs. The network manager should make these settings so that nothing changes for the user when he/she runs an application program. The print job is sent to the printer just as it's sent from a stand-alone computer.

In NetWare Lite a network printer is a printer that is connected to a server and shared by all network users. The various workstations then redirect their print jobs to this printer to be processed.

7.1 Redirecting Printer Output to the Network Printer

We already pointed out that using an application program in a NetWare Lite network (e.g., MS-WORD) is no different from running it on a stand-alone computer. The user simply selects the necessary menu item to print data.

NetWare Lite provides special commands for sending data to a specific network printer in a network. For example, at a workstation printer output to LPT1 is assigned to a specific network printer.

In NetWare Lite, such redirection of printer output is organized and managed either from the DOS prompt (NET CAPTURE) or with the NET utility program. We will explain both of these methods in the following sections.

 To be able to redirect printer output to a network printer, you must define a network printer. If you haven't done this yet, do it now. You will find detailed information about defining a network printer in Chapter 3 of this book.

7.1.1 Printer redirection with NET CAPTURE

NET CAPTURE is the faster method of redirection, because you can use this command directly from the DOS prompt.

For example, entering the following commands from the DOS prompt:

```
NET CAPTURE LPT1 LASER_S1 SERVER1 [Enter]
```

automatically redirects all printer output to LPT1 to a network printer called LASER_S1, which is connected to SERVER1.

The following message appears on the screen showing that the capture was successful:

```
Port LPT1 has been captured to Network Printer LASER_S1 on
server SERVER1.
```

NET CAPTURE provides the following settings:

Banner = Y/N

Before the actual printout, a cover sheet (banner) can be printed. This cover sheet contains information about the print job, including the name of the user who sent it.

If you do not want to have this cover sheet included in the printout, set this parameter to "n".

Default: B=N

    When you are using these parameters, simply type the first letter. For example, you could type NET CAPTURE LPT1 LASER_S1 B=Y.

Copies = number

Specifies the number of copies to be printed (from 1 to max. 250).

Default: C=1

Example: C=3

Direct = Y/N

Specifies that the output of a print job begins as soon as the first part of the print job reaches the queue. If you specify "n", then printer output does not begin until the complete print job is in the queue.

Default: D=n

Formfeed = Y/N

Specifying this parameter causes a form feed (option "y") to be executed after the printout. The paper is automatically advanced to the next page.

Default: F=y

Notify = Y/N

If you set this parameter to "y", you receive a message on the screen after the file is printed. This informs you that the file was actually printed.

Default: N=n

Papertype = 1-10

You can set the kind of paper used for the printout with this parameter. For example, this setting is practical when you want to switch between printing to continuous feed paper and printing to labels. In such cases, simply define two different formats.

Default: P=1

SETUP = String

Use this parameter to specify a control sequence for initializing the printer before starting output.

String refers to the name assigned to the control sequence. You must use the NET utility program to define the control sequence. You will find out more about this later in the chapter.

Default: S=DEFAULT

Example: S=INIT

Tabs = 0-32

Allows you to set tabs (0 to 32 spaces) in the file you are outputting. As a result, when you print, a single tab instruction is replaced by the corresponding number of spaces.

Default: T=0

Example: T=4

Wait = 0-3600

This setting specifies an interval of time (in seconds) to wait before a print job is completed (Timeout). This setting (0 to 3600 seconds) is especially practical for printing graphics, because of the waiting times that result from calculations.

Default: W=10

Example: W=360

If you would like to change any of the previous parameters from the default, you must specify it after NET CAPTURE. Simply use the first letter as a parameter name.

Place spaces in between parameters when specifying several in a row. Also, a NET CAPTURE command cancels all previous NET CAPTURE commands.

Whenever you want to redirect a user's output from an application program to a network printer, you must use NET CAPTURE. You can enable the command at the beginning of a work session, right after logging in. You don't have to enter NET CAPTURE every time you switch between programs during a work session, the capture will stay in effect until the user logs out.

Redirecting printer output with NET CAPTURE is only temporary. It remains active until you log out of the network or use NET CAPTURE DEL from the DOS prompt to cancel redirection of printer output.

7.1.2   Printer redirection with the NET utility program

NetWare Lite provides you with another option for redirecting printer output: Using the NET utility program.

Here are the steps for using NET:

1.   First call NET, and then select *Print* from the main menu.

If you are not familiar with operating the NetWare Lite menus yet, see Chapter 3 of this book. You will find detailed information there on operating this menu.

You can also call online help at any time by pressing F1 .

2.   Next, a list of the available printer ports (LPTx) appears. Using the cursor keys, select the port you would like to capture.

Users ordinarily select LPT1 here, since it's the first parallel port of your computer and the default for most application programs.

3.   After you press Enter to confirm the printer port you selected, a list of the network printers currently available appears.

4.   Select the network printer to which you want to redirect the printer output to and press Enter to confirm your choice.

Remember that only the network printers of the
                servers that are currently active will appear in the
                list. Active means that server mode (SERVER.EXE)
                has been loaded.

5.   A window showing the default settings for the capture will
        be displayed, as shown in the following figure. Here you can
        make other settings that will influence the redirection. The
        settings are identical to the parameters for the NET
        CAPTURE command.

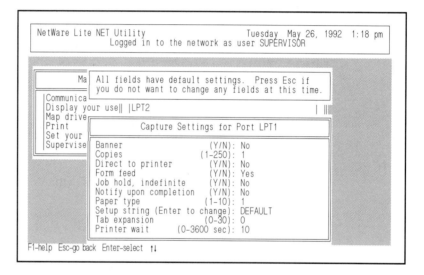

Redirecting printer output with NET

To change a setting, select the appropriate option and enter
your change.

6.   After making the settings, press ⎡Esc⎤ to complete the
        definition of printer redirection.

        The screen then displays the assignment of the network
        printer to the defined port.

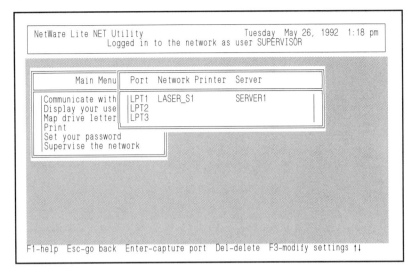

Display of the printer assignment

7. All the necessary settings have been made. You can make more settings or exit the NET utility program by pressing [Alt] [F10] and answering "Yes" to the *Exit NET* prompt.

Remember that redirecting printer output with NET is only temporary. This setting is lost when you log out of the network.

 While it is more convenient to use the NET utility program, when you're in a hurry, remember that NET CAPTURE is faster than the NET utility program.

You can also place the NET CAPTURE command in a batch file that you can call whenever you need it.

Enabling printer redirection

Necessary steps

```
NET [Enter]
Print [Enter]
Select printer port
Confirm by pressing [Enter]
Select network printer
Confirm by pressing [Enter]
Make any necessary printer settings
Press [Esc]
Press [Alt] [F10] to exit
Answer Exit prompt with "Yes"
```

7.2   Sending a Print Job to the Network Printer

The easiest method of printing a file on a network printer in NetWare Lite is to use the NET PRINT command. This command assigns a file to a queue at the DOS prompt (outside of an application program).

The files you send to the network printer with NET PRINT must either already be formatted as a print file (processed for the printer by an application program) or should be ASCII (text) files.

Before you use NET PRINT to print a file to a network printer, you must also make sure that the local port has already been captured with NET CAPTURE, as described in the previous section.

Remember: When you define a printer on any workstation (server) as a network printer, do not use it as a local printer while it is an active network printer.

If the printer got print jobs both as a network printer and a local printer simultaneously, it would result in a collision of data. To avoid this problem, address this printer as a network printer from all computers on the network, even the computer to which it is connected.

For example, to send a file named OUTPUT.TXT from the \TEXT directory on drive C: to the network printer, you would use a command similar to the following:

```
NET PRINT C:\TEXT\OUTPUT.TXT LASER_S1 [Enter]
```

If you don't specify a network printer, the NET PRINT command will print the file on the first available captured port.

After a brief interval, you will see something similar to the following message:

```
File C:\TEXT\OUTPUT.TXT has been sent to port LPT1 to be
printed on LASER_S1.
```

This tells you that the OUTPUT.TXT file was redirected to a network printer called LASER_S1.

When you specify directory and filenames for NetWare Lite commands, you can replace the DOS backslash (\) with the "regular" slash (/). You can also express the command from the preceding example in the following way:

```
NET PRINT C:/TEXT/OUTPUT.TXT Enter
```

A requirement for redirecting output to a network printer is that the printer be defined and active. Also, before you use the NET PRINT command, the local port must be redirected (NET CAPTURE).

 NET PRINT is different than the NPRINT command of NetWare 2.2 and 3.11. With NPRINT, it's not necessary to redirect printer output before an NPRINT command.

With NetWare Lite, you must redirect the output with NET CAPTURE before using NET PRINT.

7.3   Cancelling Printer Redirection

It's necessary to control printer output to a network printer from each workstation with the NET CAPTURE command. Now, it's possible that a workstation could also have a local printer connected to it. How do you print to the local printer?

If you activated redirection of printer output, there must be a way to cancel the redirection. Once again, NetWare Lite provides you with two solutions.

7.3.1   Cancelling printer redirection at the DOS prompt

NET CAPTURE has an option for cancelling redirection of printer output. The option is called DEL.

For example, if you type the following command at your workstation:

```
NET CAPTURE DEL LPT1 Enter
```

the redirection of printer output to LPT1 is cancelled, making the port operational as a local port again. The screen displays a message similar to the following:

```
Port LPT1 is no longer captured.
```

If you send a print job to LPT1, you are addressing the printer attached to port LPT1 on the workstation instead of the network printer. That means the output will be printed on the local printer, if one exists.

    As soon as a user logs out off the network, it also automatically cancels all printer redirections. In such cases, you don't need to cancel the redirection yourself.

Remember that it's not possible to print to a port on a local printer if output has been redirected with NET CAPTURE.

However, if you need to print both on the local and the network printer, you can either alternate between the two kinds of output with NET CAPTURE and NET CAPTURE DEL or reserve a port for the local printer, and use the other available ports for network printers. For example, use LPT1 for the local printer and capture LPT2 and LPT3 for network printers.

7.3.2   Cancelling printer redirection with NET

You can also cancel printer redirection with the NET utility program.

Use the following steps:

1.   After calling NET, select *Print*.

      You will see a list of the printer redirections currently active. Both the port and the assigned printer are displayed.

2.   Use the cursor keys to select the desired port.

3.   Next, press Del to cancel the printer redirection. A security prompt then appears, as shown in the following figure:

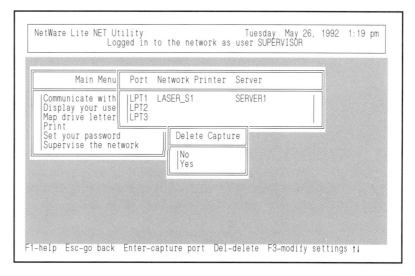

Deleting printer redirection

4.   To cancel the selected redirection, simply answer "Yes". The entry will be deleted from the window.

5.   You have just cancelled a printer redirection. You can continue making settings or exit NET by pressing [Alt] [F10] and answering "Yes" to the *Exit NET* prompt that follows.

Again, all printer output sent to this port will be sent to the local printer.

Cancelling printer redirection

Necessary steps

```
NET [Enter]
Print [Enter]
Select desired printer port
Press [Del]
Answer security prompt with "Yes"
Press [Alt] [F10] to exit
Answer exit prompt with "Yes"
```

7.4   Displaying the Current Print Jobs

Now and then it's convenient to know which print jobs are currently waiting to be printed on the individual network printers. You may wonder why your print job is taking so long.

NetWare Lite provides you with an option in the NET utility program for managing the network printers. Not only does it provide information, but you can also use this option to delete print jobs, for example.

To get general information about the print jobs assigned to a printer, use the following steps:

1. Call NET at the DOS prompt by typing:

    NET [Enter]

2. Select *Print* from the main menu of this program. A list of the defined, currently active network printers appears.

3. Now select the name of the printer for which you want additional information.

4. After you confirm your selection with [Enter], an additional window appears, as shown in the following figure:

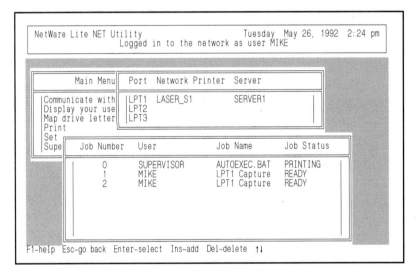

Display of the current print jobs

All print jobs currently assigned to the selected printer are displayed. The following information will be shown for each job:

Job Number

This number represents the order in which print jobs enter the queue.

User

The name of the user who sent the print job.

Job name

Name of the file to be printed. A name such as LPT1 Capture indicates that the output was sent to the captured port from an application program.

Job Status

Each print job is assigned a specific status. The following assignments are possible:

FILLING

The print job is being placed in the queue.

READY

Entire print job is in the queue waiting for assignment to the network printer.

PRINTING

Print job has been assigned to a network printer and is printing.

ON HOLD

Print job is in the queue, but it's not possible to print, since the status has been placed on "Hold".

DIRECT

Print job is being printed with the DIRECT option.

5.   To display all available information about a certain print job, select the desired job and press ⏎Enter.

      The screen will display a list similar to the one in the following figure.

    You can only display this additional information for print jobs that aren't being printed yet. Otherwise you'll get an error message.

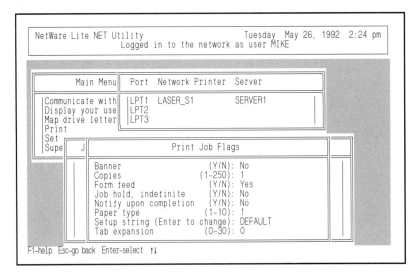

```
NetWare Lite NET Utility                    Tuesday  May 26, 1992  2:24 pm
                        Logged in to the network as user MIKE


       Main Menu  Port  Network Printer  Server
    Communicate with  LPT1  LASER_S1            SERVER1
    Display your use  LPT2
    Map drive letter  LPT3
    Print
    Set
    Supe   J                    Print Job Flags
              Banner               (Y/N): No
              Copies             (1-250): 1
              Form feed            (Y/N): Yes
              Job hold, indefinite (Y/N): No
              Notify upon completion (Y/N): No
              Paper type          (1-10): 1
              Setup string (Enter to change): DEFAULT
              Tab expansion        (0-30): 0

 F1-help  Esc-go back  Enter-select  ↑↓
```

Additional information about a print job

Here's what the items in the list mean:

Banner

Before the actual printout, a cover sheet (banner) can be printed. This cover sheet contains information about the print job, including the name of the user who sent it.

Choose *No* if you don't want to print this cover sheet.

Copies

Specifies the number of copies to be printed (from 1 to max. 250).

Form feed

Set form feed to *Yes* to execute a form feed after the printout is finished. The paper is automatically advanced to the next page. Otherwise (No) the form feed is suppressed.

Job hold, indefinite

Holds the print job until you release it again. Choose *Yes* to hold the print job. Select *No* to continue printing.

Notify upon completion

If this is set to "Yes" the user will be notified when the job has finished printing.

Paper type

Lets you specify the kind of paper used for printing. For example, this is practical when you want to switch between printing on continuous feed paper and printing to labels. Simply define two different formats and enter them here.

Setup string

Use this parameter to set a control sequence, or setup string for initializing the printer. Simply select the name that you assigned to the desired control sequence. You can also use the NET utility program to set a setup string.

Tab expansion

Specify tabs (0 to 30 spaces) here. During printout, this causes a single tab command to be replaced by the specified number of spaces.

6.   You can get information on other print jobs here by pressing `Esc` to return to the list of print jobs, and then selecting the next job and pressing `Enter`.

7.   Or, you can exit NET by pressing `Alt` `F10` and answering the *Exit NET* prompt with "Yes".

Displaying the current print jobs

Necessary steps

```
NET Enter
Print Enter
Select the desired network printer
Confirm by pressing Enter
Press Alt F10 to exit
Answer exit prompt with Yes
```

7.5   Managing Access Rights for Network Printers

Similar to managing network directories, you can also assign access rights for network printers. This gives you an option for controlling access to the network printers.

Read the next section to find out the options available for access rights for network printers.

7.5.1   Enabling access to a network printer

Before a user can print something from a network printer, the right to access a network printer must be granted.

Although this automatically happens when you set up a new network printer, we'd like to show you the steps. You may have to do this yourself sometime.

Here are the steps for changing the default access rights (valid for all users):

1.   First call the NET utility program and select *Supervise the network*.

2.   Next, select *Network printers* from the submenu that appears. A list of the defined network printers appears.

☞   You can read about how to set up new network printers in Chapter 3 of this book. A network printer that is installed for the first time is automatically assigned the ALL access right.

3.   Select the name of the network printer whose default access rights you want to change.

4.   Press (Enter) to confirm your selection. A window with additional information on the selected printer appears:

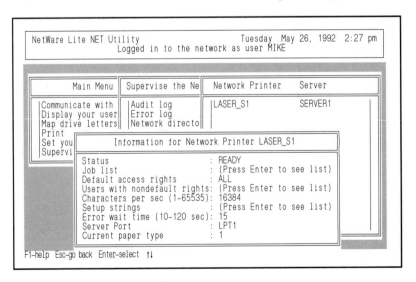

Information on the selected network printer

5. To change the default access right, select the *Default access rights* option and press (Enter).

    Another window appears listing the available access rights:

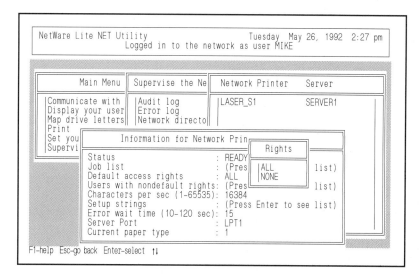

```
NetWare Lite NET Utility                    Tuesday  May 26, 1992  2:27 pm
                  Logged in to the network as user MIKE

      Main Menu    Supervise the Ne  Network Printer    Server

 Communicate with   Audit log        LASER_S1             SERVER1
 Display your user  Error log
 Map drive letters  Network directo
 Print
 Set you          Information for Network Prin          Rights
 Supervi
         Status                   : READY
         Job list                 : (Pres  ALL          list)
         Default access rights    : ALL    NONE
         Users with nondefault rights: (Pres            list)
         Characters per sec (1-65535): 16384
         Setup strings            : (Press Enter to see list)
         Error wait time (10-120 sec): 15
         Server Port              : LPT1
         Current paper type       : 1

 F1-help  Esc-go back  Enter-select  ↑↓
```

Selection of access rights

6. From this window, select the access right that you want to assign to the selected network printer as the default access right.

   When you assign access rights for a network printer, you can only choose between two alternatives, ALL or NONE. If you select NONE, no user will have access to the printer. Selecting ALL specifies that all network users have access to the printer.

    Additional information about how to change the nondefault access rights of users is discussed in the next section.

7. After you press (Enter) to confirm your selection, the selected access right appears in the window next to the *Default access rights* setting.

8. Press (Esc) to exit this window. This returns you to the list of available network printers.

9. You can make further settings or exit NET by pressing (Alt) (F10) and answering the *Exit NET* prompt with "Yes".

You have just set the default access rights for a network printer. In the next section we'll show you how to assign nondefault access rights.

Enabling access to a network printer

Necessary steps

```
NET (Enter)
Supervise the network (Enter)
Network printers (Enter)
Select desired Network printer
Confirm your selection with (Enter)
Select Default access rights (Enter)
Select the desired option
Confirm by pressing (Enter)
Press (Esc)
Press (Alt) (F10) to exit
Answer Exit NET prompt with "Yes"
```

7.5.2 Changing the nondefault access rights

After assigning default access rights to a network printer, we'd like to show you how to change these rights for individual users.

Let's suppose you assigned a default access right of NONE to a network printer. This means that none of the network users has access to this printer. In other words, no one can use this printer.

NetWare Lite also has an option for granting a particular user the right to print something on this printer. This is called assigning nondefault access rights (*Users with nondefault rights*).

Nondefault access rights differ from default access rights for the printer. Nondefault access rights always refer to an individual user, while default access rights are valid for all users.

Here are the steps necessary for assigning a user nondefault access rights for a network printer:

1. First, load the NET utility program.

2. Next, select *Supervise the network* from the main menu of this program and press (Enter).

3. A submenu appears with a menu item called *Network printers*. Select this item and press (Enter) to display a list of defined network printers.

4. Select the name of the network printer for which you want to assign nondefault access rights.

5. Now press (Enter) to confirm your selection. An additional window appears with information about the network printer you just selected.

6. Select the *Users with nondefault rights* option.

7. After you press (Enter), a list of those users who already have been assigned nondefault access rights appears.

    If nondefault access rights haven't been assigned for the network printer, then the list will be empty. If the user is already in the list, simply move the highlight to the name and continue with step 10.

8. Next, press (Ins) to display a list of the defined usernames, as shown in the following figure.

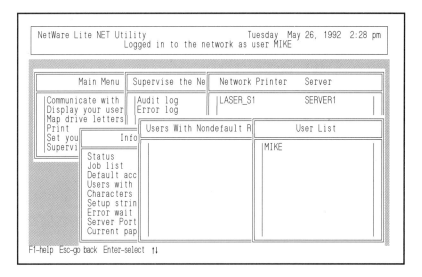

Display of the available usernames

9. From this list, select the name of the user for which you want to assign nondefault access rights for the printer.

10. After you confirm your selection by pressing (Enter), another window appears listing the possible access rights.

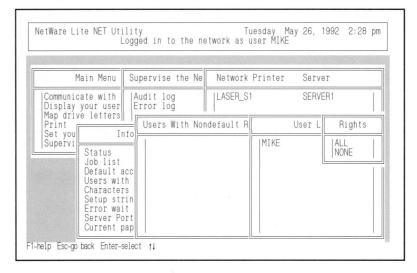

Selection of access rights

11.   From this window, select the access right you want to assign to the selected user as the nondefault access right for the network printer.

        If you would like the user to be able to access the network printer, select ALL.

12.   The selected username and the assigned access right then appear on the screen, as shown in the following figure:

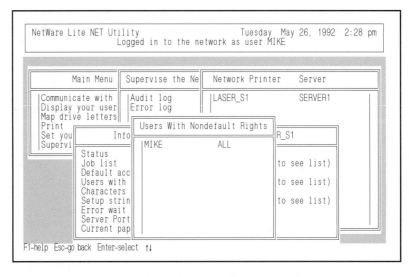

Username and assigned access right

To assign nondefault access rights for the selected network printer to other users, simply press (Ins) again and repeat the procedure.

13.   Press (Esc) to exit the list of usernames with nondefault access rights.

If you exit NET at this time by pressing (Alt) (F10), all the changes you made will be lost.

14.   To save the new settings, press (Esc) again, which returns you to the list of the available network printers.

15.   Now you can make further settings or exit NET safely by pressing (Alt) (F10) and answering the *Exit NET* prompt with "Yes".

You have just performed the steps necessary for assigning nondefault access rights to a network printer. The newly assigned rights will be valid the next time the user logs in on the network.

Changing the nondefault access rights for a network printer

Necessary steps

```
NET (Enter)
Supervise the network (Enter)
Network printers (Enter)
Select the desired network printer and press (Enter)
Users with nondefault rights (Enter)
Select the desired username (Ins)
Confirm by pressing (Enter)
Select nondefault access rights
Confirm by pressing (Enter)
Press (Esc) twice
Press (Alt) (F10) to exit
Answer Exit NET prompt with "Yes"
```

7.5.3 Removing access to a network printer from a single user

In the last section you learned how to change the nondefault access rights of single users. In the next two sections, we'd like to discuss two special cases.

In this section, we'll discuss how to remove a single user's access to a network printer. The principle is based on assigning ALL as the default access right and NONE as the users nondefault access right.

Here are the steps:

1.   Call the NET utility program from the DOS prompt with:

      NET (Enter)

2.   Then select *Supervise the network* from the main menu and press (Enter).

3.   From the *Supervise the network* menu, select *Network printers* and press (Enter). A list of the defined network printers then appears.

4.   Choose the name of the printer for which you want to remove access from the user, and press (Enter). An additional window appears with more information about the selected network printer.

5.   Select the *Default access rights* option and press (Enter).

      Another window appears showing the available access rights:

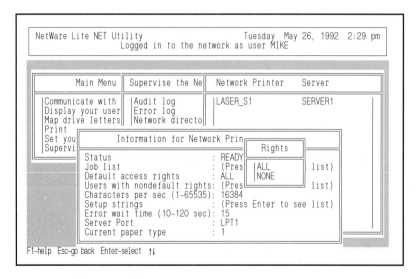

Selection of access rights

6.   Select ALL from the list to assign this right to the selected network printer as default access right.

7.   After pressing [Enter] to confirm your selection, you return to the display of information about the selected network printer.

8.   The *Users with nondefault rights* option will now be highlighted. Press [Enter] to select this option.

        Next, you see a list of users who have nondefault access rights for this network printer.

☞   If nondefault access rights haven't been assigned for this network printer, then the list will be empty.

9.   If the name of the user whose access you want to remove appears in this list, select this username and press [Enter]. Then continue with step 11.

        If the username does not appear in this list, first press [Ins] to display a list of all usernames known to the network:

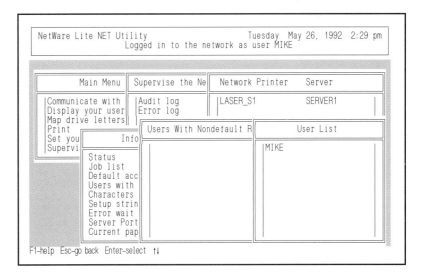

```
NetWare Lite NET Utility                    Tuesday  May 26, 1992  2:29 pm
                    Logged in to the network as user MIKE

        Main Menu    Supervise the Ne   Network Printer    Server
  Communicate with  Audit log         |LASER_S1          SERVER1
  Display your user Error log
  Map drive letters
  Print              Info  Users With Nondefault R         User List
  Set you       Info
  Supervi  Status                              |MIKE
           Job list
           Default acc
           Users with
           Characters
           Setup strin
           Error wait
           Server Port
           Current pap

F1-help  Esc-go back  Enter-select  ↑↓
```

Display of available usernames

10.   From this list, select the name of the user whose access to the selected network printer you want to remove and press [Enter].

11.   A window will appear showing the available access rights. Select NONE and press [Enter] to remove the user's access.

12.   You will then be returned to the list of usernames and assigned access rights.

If you exit NET here by pressing [Alt] [F10], all the settings will be lost.

13.   Now press [Esc] twice to exit the list and save the settings you have just made.

14.   This returns you to the list of available network printers, where you can make further settings or exit NET safely by pressing [Alt] [F10] and answering the *Exit NET* prompt with "Yes".

Follow these steps to remove a single user's access to a network printer. In the next section we'll show you how to restrict access to a network printer to a single user.

Removing a single user's access to a network printer

Necessary steps

```
NET [Enter]
Supervise the network [Enter]
Network printers [Enter]
Select the desired network printer and press [Enter]
Select the Default access rights option and press [Enter]
Select ALL and press [Enter]
Select the Users with nondefault rights option and press [Enter]
Select the desired username and press [Enter]
Select NONE and press [Enter]
Press [Esc] twice
Press [Alt] [F10] to exit
Answer exit prompt with Yes
```

7.5.4   Limiting access to a network printer to a single user

In the last section you learned how to remove a single user's access to a network printer. In this section you will learn how to restrict access for a network printer to a single user.

The network printer is assigned NONE as the default access right, while the user is assigned a nondefault right of ALL.

The following steps are necessary for this:

1.   Call NET from the DOS prompt with:

        NET [Enter]

2.   Then select *Supervise the network* from the main menu and press Enter.

3.   From the *Supervise the network* menu, select *Network printers* and press Enter. A list of the defined network printers will then appear.

4.   Choose the name of the network printer that you only want one user to be able to access, and press Enter. An additional window appears with more information about the selected printer.

5.   Select the *Default access rights* option and press Enter. Another window appears listing the available access rights.

6.   Select NONE from this window and press Enter. This assigns NONE as the default access right for the selected network printer. You will then be returned to the window showing information about the selected network printer.

7.   The *Users with nondefault access rights* option will now be highlighted. Press Enter to select this option.

     Next, a list of users with nondefault access rights for this network printer appears.

☞   If nondefault access rights haven't been assigned for the network printer, then this list will be empty.

8.   If the name of the user you want to have access appears in this list, select this username and confirm by pressing Enter. Then continue with step 11.

     If the username is not in this list, press Ins to display a list of all usernames known to the network.

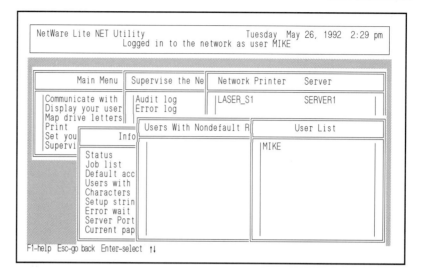

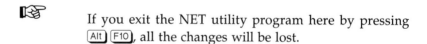

Display of available usernames

9.   Now select the name of the user that you want to have access to the selected network printer from this list and press Enter.

10.   Next you see a screen display of the available access rights.

11.   Select the ALL option and confirm by pressing Enter.

        Then you return to the list of usernames and assigned access rights.

☞   If you exit the NET utility program here by pressing Alt F10, all the changes will be lost.

12.   Now press Esc twice to exit the window and save the changes you just made.

13.   You return to the list of available network printers, where you can make further settings or exit NET safely by pressing Alt F10 and answering the *Exit NET* prompt with "Yes".

You have just learned a method for limiting access to a network printer to a single user.

Limiting access to a network printer to a single user

Necessary steps

```
NET [Enter]
Supervise the network [Enter]
Network printers [Enter]
Select desired Network printers and press [Enter]
Select Default access rights option and press [Enter]
Select NONE and confirm by pressing [Enter]
Select Users with nondefault rights option and press [Enter]
Select desired username and press [Enter]
Select ALL and confirm by pressing [Enter]
Press [Esc] twice
Press [Alt] [F10] to exit
Answer Exit NET prompt with "Yes"
```

7.5.5   Information about nondefault access rights

As the user of a network, it's important that you be informed at all times about your assigned access rights for the network printers. This way you always know which printer you can print to.

NetWare Lite has a command that you can use at the DOS prompt to get the desired information.

If you are logged in to the network, simply enter the following command:

```
NET NPLIST [Enter]
```

Then you will see a list similar to the following:

```
Network printer      Server            Rights
==============       =======           ======

LASER_S1             SERVER1           ALL

Total network printers: 1
```

This list provides you with information about the network printers currently available and the last column also contains information about your nondefault access rights.

These are the rights the Supervisor assigned to you for accessing the network printer.

7.5.6   Temporarily ending access to a network printer

If you need to do maintenance work on a network printer, then you should make sure that no user can access the printer during this time.

If a network printer is not in operation and print jobs are still sent to it, these print jobs are collected in the queue.

To end access to a network printer for a limited period of time, assign the network printer the default access right NONE.

     Instead of temporarily "locking" access to a network printer, you could also delete the network printer from the list of available network printers. However, if this is done you would have to completely re-install the network printer after you finished the work.

With the solution we introduce to you here, simply re-assign the default access right ALL to the printer to re-enable access to the printer.

To temporarily suppress access to a network printer, you need to take the following steps:

1.   Call NET from the DOS prompt with:

      NET (Enter)

2.   Then select *Supervise the network* from the main menu and press (Enter).

3.   From the *Supervise the network* menu, select *Network printers* and press (Enter). A list of the defined network printers will appear.

4.   Select the name of the network printer for which you want to temporarily remove access, and press (Enter). An additional window appears with more information about the selected printer.

     If the *Default access rights* entry is NONE, it means that the default access rights for this network printer have already been removed. In such a case, you may simply press (Esc) to exit this window.

5.   Select the *Default access rights* option and press (Enter). Another window appears listing the available access rights.

6. To assign the access right NONE to the selected printer, select the option NONE and confirm your selection by pressing ⌷Enter⌷.

7. The selected access right appears in the additional window of the selected network printer, as shown in the following figure:

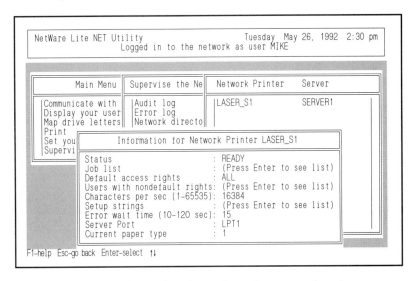

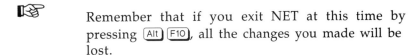

Display of additional information of a network printer

☞ Remember that if you exit NET at this time by pressing ⌷Alt⌷ ⌷F10⌷, all the changes you made will be lost.

8. To be sure that the settings are saved, press ⌷Esc⌷ to return to the list of available network directories.

9. Now you can make further changes or exit NET safely by pressing ⌷Alt⌷ ⌷F10⌋ and answering the *Exit NET* prompt with "Yes".

You have just temporarily suppressed access to the selected network printer for all users of the network. Remember to restore the original state after performing the maintenance work by re-assigning the printer the default access right of ALL.

Temporarily suppressing access to a network printer

Necessary steps

```
NET Enter
Supervise the network Enter
Network printers Enter
Select the desired network printer and press Enter
Select the Default access rights option and press Enter
Select NONE and confirm by pressing Enter
Press Esc
Press Alt F10 to exit
Answer exit prompt with "Yes"
```

7.6   Deleting Print Jobs From the Queue

If you send print jobs to the printer and then discover that certain jobs aren't properly prepared, you can remove these print jobs from the queue, before they are printed. You can only do this while the print jobs are still in the queue. After the jobs leave the queue, this is no longer possible. Here are the steps necessary for deleting a print job from the queue of a network printer:

1.   Call NET at the DOS prompt with:

      NET Enter

2.   Select the *Print* option from the main menu and press Enter. A list of the defined, currently active network printers appears.

3.   Select the name of the printer from whose queue you want to delete a print job.

4.   After you press Enter to confirm your selection, an additional window appears with a list of the current print jobs.

5.   Now use the cursor keys to select the print job you want to delete.

6.   Next, simply press Del, causing the following security prompt to appear:

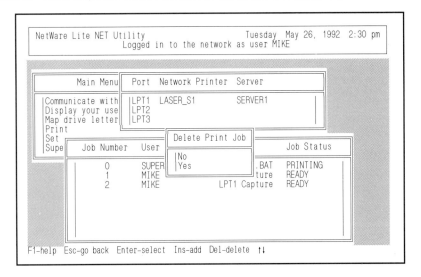

```
 NetWare Lite NET Utility                Tuesday May 26, 1992  2:30 pm
                Logged in to the network as user MIKE

 ┌──────────────┬──────────────────────────────────────────────┐
 │   Main Menu  │ Port  Network Printer  Server                 │
 ├──────────────┤ LPT1  LASER_S1         SERVER1                │
 │Communicate with LPT2                                         │
 │Display your use LPT3                                         │
 │Map drive letter                                             │
 │Print         ┌────────────────┐                             │
 │Set           │ Delete Print Job │                           │
 │Supe  Job Number  User │ No                    Job Status     │
 │                       │ Yes                                  │
 │         0    SUPER                        .BAT   PRINTING    │
 │         1    MIKE                         ture   READY       │
 │         2    MIKE              LPT1 Capture      READY       │
 │                                                              │
 │                                                              │
 │                                                              │
 └──────────────────────────────────────────────────────────────┘
 F1-help  Esc-go back  Enter-select  Ins-add  Del-delete  ↑↓
```

Security prompt when you delete

☞ A print job that is already sent to the printer (status PRINTING) can no longer be deleted.

7. Answer the Delete print job prompt with "Yes" to delete the selected print job.

8. Now you can make further settings or exit NET by pressing Alt F10 and answering "Yes" to the exit prompt that follows.

You have just learned how to delete one or more print jobs from a queue. In the next section we'll show you how to hold a print job.

Deleting print jobs

Necessary steps

```
NET Enter
Print Enter
Select the desired network printer and confirm by pressing Enter
Select the desired print job
Press Del
Answer Delete print job prompt with "Yes"
Press Alt F10 to exit
Answer exit prompt with "Yes"
```

7.7   Holding a Print Job Temporarily

In the last section you learned how to remove print jobs from a queue. This procedure is valuable whenever you send print jobs and then discover that there's a mistake somewhere (for example, if you discover spelling errors in a document file).

However, you can also hold a print job temporarily, for later printing. In this case, you must set the *Job hold, indefinite* box to *Yes* in the additional window of the print job.

Here are the steps necessary for holding a print job:

1.   Call NET from the DOS prompt with:

      NET Enter

2.   Then select *Print* in the main menu to display a list of the defined, currently active network printers.

3.   Choose the name of the printer in whose queue a print job is to be held.

4.   After you confirm your choice by pressing Enter, an additional window appears, in which the current print jobs are displayed.

5.   Now use the cursor keys to select the print job that is to be held and confirm it by pressing Enter. An additional window appears with information on the selected print job.

☞   You cannot make changes to a print job that has already been sent to the printer (status PRINTING).

6.   Select the *Job hold, indefinite* option.

7.   Press Y to select "Yes".

8.   After pressing Enter, you can exit the window by pressing Esc.

   Next, you return to the list of print jobs. The selected print job is on HOLD (Job Status - Holding).

9.   You can make further settings or exit NET by pressing Alt F10 and answering "Yes" to the exit prompt that follows.

You have just placed a print job on hold. You must release the job again before it will be sent to the network printer (Set *Job hold, indefinite* to *No*).

Placing printer output on hold temporarily

Necessary steps

```
NET Enter
Print Enter
Select the desired network printer and press Enter
Select the desired print job and press Enter
Select the Job hold, indefinite option
Press Y
Confirm by pressing Enter
Press Esc
Press Alt F10 to exit
Answer exit prompt with "Yes"
```

7.8 Displaying All Available Network Printers

NetWare Lite also provides you with an option for determining which network printers are currently available. This setting applies to the current server, and to all network printers defined (and active) anywhere within the network.

Displaying available network printers can be useful if you send a print job to the printer, but nothing prints. In such a case, it's possible that either the network printer has been deleted or the server hasn't been loaded yet.

To display the available network printers, enter the following command at the DOS prompt:

```
NET NPLIST Enter
```

You will see a list of network printers similar to the following example:

```
Network printers     Servers       Rights
=================     =======       ======

LASER_S1             SERVER1       ALL
LABEL_S2             SERVER2       NONE

Total network printers: 2
```

This list identifies all network printers that are defined in the network and are currently loaded.

You load network printers by calling SERVER.EXE to
enable server mode on the server the network printer is
connected to.

A list, similar to the one displayed here, could be
incomplete if SERVER.EXE has not yet been loaded on
all servers in the network.

7.9   Deleting a Network Printer

From time to time you may have to completely delete a defined
network printer.

     When you delete a network printer, all of its
information is also deleted. For example, the access
rights are deleted. Also, any print jobs that are still in
the printer queue are also deleted.

Therefore, be extremely careful when you delete a
network printer.

Use the following procedure to delete a network printer:

1.   Call the NET utility program from the DOS prompt with:

     NET [Enter]

2.   Now select *Supervise the network* option in the main menu
     and press [Enter].

3.   Select *Network printers* from the submenu that appears and
     press [Enter] to display a list of the defined network printers.

4.   In this list, use the cursor keys to select the network printer
     that you want to delete.

5.   Now simply press [Del], and answer "Yes" to the *Delete
     Network Printer* prompt.

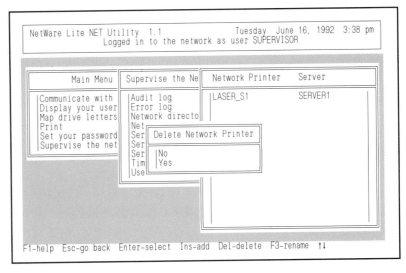

Security prompt that appears when you delete a network printer

6.   After deleting the printer, you return to the list of available network printers.

7.   You can now make further settings or exit NET by pressing [Alt] [F10] and answering the *Exit NET* prompt with "Yes".

You have just deleted a network printer. As we mentioned earlier, you should be very careful when deleting network printers.

Deleting a network printer

Necessary steps

```
NET [Enter]
Supervise the network [Enter]
Network printers [Enter]
Select the desired network printer
Press [Del]
Answer Delete Network Printer prompt with "Yes"
Press [Alt] [F10] to exit
Answer exit prompt with "Yes"
```

7.10   Redirecting Output to LPT2

To redirect output from the second parallel port (LPT2) to a specific network printer, you can use the NET CAPTURE command at the DOS prompt.

For example, you could use the following command:

```
NET CAPTURE LPT2 LASER_S2 SERVER2 [Enter]
```

You will then see the following message on the screen:

```
Output to LPT2 has been redirected to network printer
LASER_S2 on Server SERVER2.
```

This command assigns the network printer LASER_S2 to LPT2.
Beginning immediately, all output to LPT2 will be automatically
redirected to the network printer LASER_S2.

      Remember that with NetWare Lite, you can also
assign a network printer to more than one printer port.

7.11 Current Information About NET CAPTURE

After redirecting several printer ports, you can easily "lose track"
of things. For example, you might not remember what you assigned
to whom.

NetWare Lite also has a solution for this problem.

Entering the following command at the DOS prompt gives you
detailed information about the current settings of NET CAPTURE.
Here's an example of what the information might look like:

```
NET CAPTURE [Enter]

                   Current Captured Local Ports
   Local Port    Network Printer    Server    Capture Settings
   ==========    ===============    ======    ================

   LPT1          LASER_S1           SERVER1   Banner=N
                                              Papertype=1
                                              Hold=N
                                              Setup=DEFAULT
                                              Copies=1 Tabs=0
                                              Formfeed=Y
                                              Direct=N Wait=10
                                              Notify=N
```

You can get information about the printer ports and their current
assignments from this list. You find the values here for the
parameters that you can use when you enable the printer
redirection.

8.   Communication With NetWare Lite

Communication within your network is very important, especially when there are many workstations that are far away from each other. NetWare Lite provides various options for electronic communication. You will be able to easily send messages to any of the users logged in to the network.

Electronic mail capabilities with NetWare Lite (whether you're a normal user or the network supervisor) are discussed in this chapter. We'll show you how to send messages using the NET utility program and the NET SEND command.

8.1   Sending a Message With NET

The NET utility offers a quick way to send brief messages from one network user to another. The menu system of this program makes it very easy for all network users to use. In the following section we'll discuss how to send messages with NET.

8.1.1   Sending a message to all active users

The utility program NET allows you to send a message to all users that are currently logged in to the network.

Follow these steps:

1.   Start the NET utility program from the operating system with:

        NET [Enter]

         If you need information on how to select and activate menu functions under NetWare Lite, refer to Chapter 3.

2.   Select the *Communicate with users* item from the main menu and press [Enter].

3.   From the *Communicate with Users* menu, select *Send messages* and press [Enter].

4.   A list of the users currently connected to the network will then appear, as shown in the following screen. To send a message to all users currently logged in to the network, select the *ALL CONNECTED USERS* option and press [Enter].

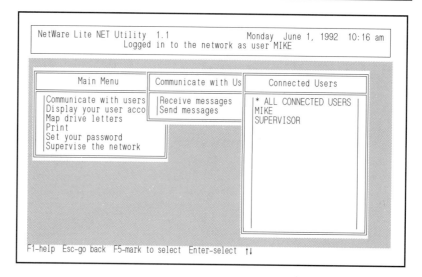

Sending a message to all users

5.   An input line, on which you can enter your message, will
       appear. Type in your message. It can contain a maximum of
       30 characters.

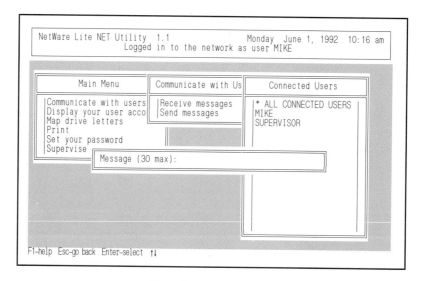

Entering a message

6.   Press ⌑Enter⌑ and the message will be sent to all users currently
       logged in to the network.

       The message will appear on line 25 of each of the
       user's workstation. Each user must press ⌑Ctrl⌑ ⌑Enter⌑ to
       clear the message and continue working.

The message has now been sent. You can continue working within NET or exit by pressing [Alt] [F10] and answering "Yes" to the prompt that follows.

Sending a message to all network users

Necessary steps

```
NET [Enter]
Communicate with users [Enter]
Send Messages [Enter]
ALL CONNECTED USERS [Enter]
Enter the message and press [Enter]
Press [Alt] [F10] to exit
Answer Exit NET prompt with "Yes"
```

8.1.2 Sending a message to a single user

The NET utility also allows you to send a message to a single user on the network.

Follow these steps:

1. Start the NET utility program from the operating system with:

    NET [Enter]

2. Select the *Communicate with users* item from the main menu and press [Enter].

3. From the *Communicate with Users* menu, select *Send messages* and press [Enter].

4. A list of the users currently connected to the network will then appear. Use the cursor keys to select the user to which you want to send the message and press [Enter].

  A message can only be sent to a user that is logged in to the network. If the user's name is not in this list, you will have to wait until the user logs in to send the message.

You can also select several users simultaneously by using [F5] to make a multiple selection (refer to Chapter 3).

5.   An input line, on which you can enter your message, will appear. Type in your message. It can contain a maximum of 30 characters.

6.   When you press [Enter], the message will be sent to the selected user.

The message will appear on line 25 of each of the user's workstation. Each user must press [Ctrl] [Enter] to clear the message and continue working.

The message has now been sent. You can continue working within NET or exit by pressing [Alt] [F10] and answering "Yes" to the prompt that follows.

Sending a message to a single user

Necessary steps

```
NET [Enter]
Communicate with users [Enter]
Send Messages [Enter]
Select the desired user name and press [Enter]
Enter the message and press [Enter]
Press [Alt] [F10] to exit
Answer Exit NET prompt with "Yes"
```

8.2   Sending a Message With NET SEND

In addition to the NET utility, you can also use the NET SEND command to send a message over the network. This command can be used to send a short note or message to another user. For example, to send a message to the user MIKE, a command, such as the following, could be entered from the operating system prompt:

```
NET SEND "I'm waiting for those copies!!" MIKE [Enter]
```

The user MIKE will then receive this message on the screen in line 25 (the bottom line of the screen). Your user name will automatically be attached to the message so that the receiver knows who sent it.

The message can contain a maximum of 30 characters. The text of the message must be enclosed in quotation marks. The following shows the general syntax of the NET SEND command:

```
NET SEND "message" username
```

If you try to send a message to a user that is not logged in, you'll receive an error message similar to the following:

```
MIKE is not a connected user. Run NET ULIST fo find connected users.
```

This means that the user you're trying to reach is not logged in. You'll have to try again at a later time.

     You may use the NET ULIST command to display a list of the currently connected users. Type the command as follows at the DOS prompt:

```
NET ULIST  Enter
```

You may then send a message to any of the users listed.

To send the same message to more than one user, simply enter the user names separated by spaces:

```
NET SEND "Sales meeting in 20 minutes" SHERI MIKE  Enter
```

Both users SHERI and MIKE will receive the following message on their screens:

```
"Sales meeting in 20 minutes"
```

The last option for the NET SEND command is sending a message to all users. Use the option ALL as shown in the following example:

```
NET SEND "Server shutting down" ALL  Enter
```

8.3   Clearing a Message From the Screen

With NetWare Lite you must clear the message before you can continue working. To clear a message from your screen after you've read it, you should press the following keys:

```
Ctrl   Enter
```

     You won't be able to continue working on your workstation until you've cleared the message from your screen.

The message will be removed from your screen and you'll be able to continue with your work.

8.4   Switching the Message Display On and Off

NetWare Lite provides two commands for switching the message display on and off. These commands will affect messages that were sent with the NET SEND command or NET utility.

8.4.1   Suppressing messages from other workstations

The NET RECEIVE command allows you to suppress the display of messages. This is helpful if you're working in an application program and you don't want to be interrupted by messages on your screen. To switch off the display of messages that are sent from other workstations, enter:

```
NET RECEIVE OFF (Enter)
```

Now any messages sent to you from other workstations will no longer be displayed, as indicated by the message that will appear on your screen:

```
Messages sent to your workstation will NOT appear on your
monitor.
```

       The NET RECEIVE OFF command will remain active until you restart the workstation or until you execute the NET RECEIVE ON command.

8.4.2   Activating the display of messages

To switch on the display of messages, enter the NET RECEIVE command at the operating system level as follows:

```
NET RECEIVE ON (Enter)
```

The following message will indicate the result of this command:

```
Messages sent to your computer will appear on your
monitor.
```

8.4.3   Influencing the display of messages with NET

You can also use the NET utility to turn the display of messages on and off. Please use the following procedure to enable/disable the display of messages:

1.   Start the NET utility from the DOS prompt, with:

```
NET (Enter)
```

2. Select the *Communicate with users* option from the main menu and press Enter.

3. You should then select the *Receive messages* item from the *Communicate with Users* menu and press Enter.

4. A menu listing the available reception options will then appear as follows:

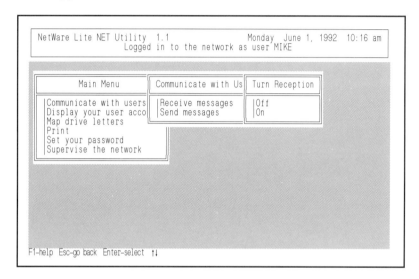

```
NetWare Lite NET Utility  1.1                Monday  June 1, 1992  10:16 am
                    Logged in to the network as user MIKE

        Main Menu          Communicate with Us  Turn Reception
   Communicate with users   Receive messages     Off
   Display your user acco    Send messages        On
   Map drive letters
   Print
   Set your password
   Supervise the network





   F1-help  Esc-go back  Enter-select  ↑↓
```

Turning message reception on/off

5. If you would like to suppress the display of messages, select the *OFF* option and press Enter.

   To enable the display of messages, select the *ON* option and press Enter.

6. The display of messages has now been turned on or off. You may continue working within NET or press Alt F10 to exit.

 The suppression of messages setting will remain active until you restart the workstation or until you re-enable the display of messages.

Influencing the display of messages

Necessary steps

```
NET Enter
Communicate with users Enter
Receive messages Enter
Select the desired option and press Enter
Press Alt F10 to exit NET
Answer Exit prompt with "Yes"
```

9. The Supervisor

We have already mentioned several times that there is one user among the users of a network who has special privileges and power over all the other users. This user is called the supervisor. A supervisor is a person who takes care of all the important management tasks within a network and sees to it that users are able to work smoothly. A supervisor is always there to handle any problems that might arise. This chapter deals with some of the special tasks of a supervisor.

By granting supervisor privleges (see Chapter 5), the supervisor can determine that a user will have the same rights (and duties) as the supervisor.

9.1 Inspecting the Error Log of the Network

If serious errors occur in the network that you (the supervisor) can't solve, you may be able to get some help by inspecting the error log of the network. For example, when print jobs cannot be printed because a network printer hasn't been switched on or for some other reason, a status report will appear in the error log. NetWare Lite automatically writes such information to the error log. To inspect this file, use the following steps:

1. Call the NET utility program by typing the following at the DOS prompt:

   NET [Enter]

2. Then select *Supervise the network* from the main menu of NET and press [Enter].

If you still aren't familiar with operating the NetWare Lite menus, read Chapter 3 of this book. You will find detailed information about operating these menus there.

You can also call online help at any time by pressing [F1].

3. From the *Supervise the Network* menu, select *Error log* and press [Enter]. You will then see the following menu display:

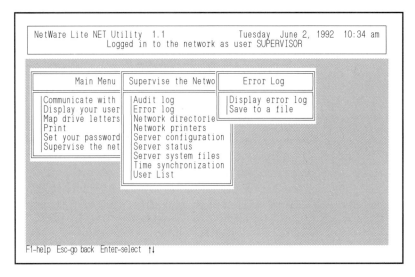

Display of the error log

4.   Next, select *Display error log* and press Enter. The current
contents of the error log appear on the screen:

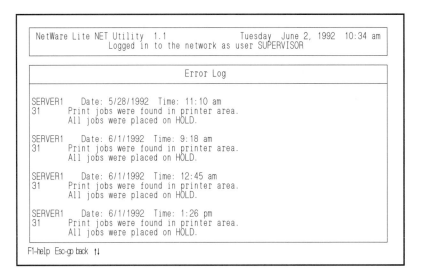

Contents of the error log

You may be able to find information in the error log that
will help you solve your problem.

        If there are no errors recorded in this file, a message
informing you of this appears on the screen and you
automatically return to *Error Log* menu.

5.   When you press ⟨Esc⟩ to exit the display of the error log, a prompt appears on the screen, asking whether you want to delete the contents of the file. Answer Yes only when you are sure that you don't need any of the information contained in this error log.

    From time to time you will have to delete the error log, since it would otherwise grow much too large and cluttered.

6.   From the *Error log* menu you can exit NET by pressing ⟨Alt⟩ ⟨F10⟩ and answering the *Exit NET* prompt with "Yes".

Now you know how to inspect the error log of the network. In the next section we'll show you how to save the contents of an error log to a file.

Displaying the error log

Necessary steps

```
NET ⟨Enter⟩
Supervise the network ⟨Enter⟩
Error log ⟨Enter⟩
Display error log ⟨Enter⟩
View contents of the error log
Press ⟨Esc⟩
Answer security prompt with Yes or No
Press ⟨Alt⟩ ⟨F10⟩ to exit
Answer exit prompt with Yes
```

9.2   Saving the System Error Log

In the last section you learned how to display the contents of the error log. In this section we show you how to save those contents in a separate file. You can view the contents of this file with any Editor or by using the TYPE command at the DOS prompt.

The following steps are necessary for saving the error log to a file:

1.   Call NET from the DOS prompt with:

    NET ⟨Enter⟩

2.   Select the *Supervise the network* option from the main menu and press ⟨Enter⟩.

3.   In the submenu that appears, select *Error log* and press ⟨Enter⟩.

4.   Select the *Save to a file* option from the *Error Log* menu. An input line allowing you to specify the path for the file will appear, as shown in the following figure:

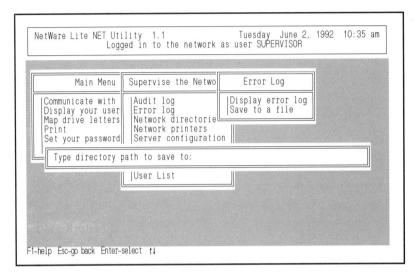

```
NetWare Lite NET Utility  1.1                Tuesday  June 2, 1992  10:35 am
                  Logged in to the network as user SUPERVISOR


        ┌────────Main Menu────────┐┌─Supervise the Netwo─┐┌──────Error Log──────┐
        │Communicate with         ││Audit log            ││Display error log    │
        │Display your user         ││Error log            ││Save to a file       │
        │Map drive letters         ││Network directorie──┘└─────────────────────┘
        │Print                    ││Network printers     │
        │Set your password         ││Server configuration │
        └─────────┌─Type directory path to save to:─────────────────────────────┐
                  └──────────────────────────────────────────────────────────────┘
                   │User List            │
                   └─────────────────────┘



F1-help  Esc-go back  Enter-select  ↑↓
```

Saving the contents of the error log to a file

5.   You must specify the name of the drive and directory in which the error log is to be placed. Specify a name, such as C:\NWLITE. It is not neccessary to enter a filename, NetWare Lite will save the contents of the error log in a file named ERROR.LOG.

    You must specify a directory that already exists (e.g., \NWLITE).

The contents of the error log are saved to a file called ERROR.LOG.

6.   After pressing Enter to confirm the path you entered, the file will be saved. After a short time, a message appears on the screen to inform you of this.

Then a security prompt appears on the screen asking whether you want to delete the error log:

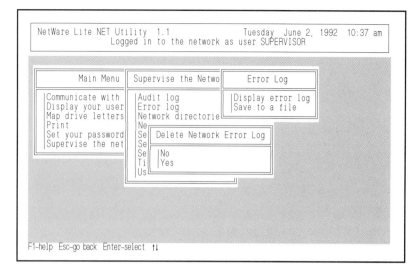

Deleting the error log

The deletion affects the current error log that is managed by NetWare Lite. The file you just saved is not deleted.

7.   After answering the prompt, you return to the *Error log* menu. You can exit NET from there by pressing Alt F10 and answering the exit prompt with "Yes".

You have just saved an error log to a file. You can edit this file, called ERROR.LOG, since the data is in a text (ASCII) format.

Saving the error log

Necessary steps

```
NET Enter
Supervise the network Enter
Error log Enter
Save to a file Enter
Enter the desired path and press
Confirm by pressing Enter
Answer Delete Network Error Log prompt with Yes or No
Press Alt F10 to exit
Answer Exit NET prompt with Yes
```

9.3   Recording Activities on the Network

Along with the error log, there is another system file, called an
audit log. NetWare Lite allows you to make entries in this file to
keep track of activities on the network.

Here are the steps necessary for displaying the contents of this log
file on the screen:

1.   Call the NET utility program from the DOS prompt with:

      NET (Enter)

2.   Then select the *Supervise the network* option and press
      (Enter).

3.   From the submenu that appears, select the *Audit log* menu
      item and press (Enter). You will then see the following menu
      display:

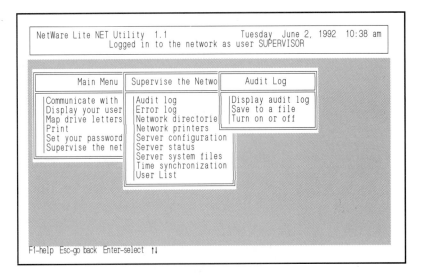

Display of the audit log

4.   Next, select *Display audit log* and press (Enter) to display
      the current contents of the audit log:

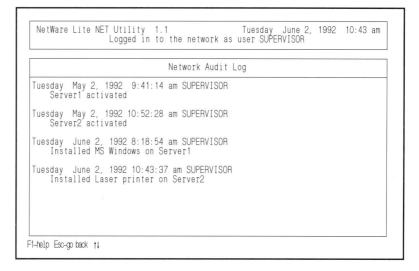

```
┌─────────────────────────────────────────────────────────────────────┐
│ ┌───────────────────────────────────────────────────────────────┐   │
│ │ NetWare Lite NET Utility  1.1              Tuesday  June 2, 1992  10:43 am │
│ │                 Logged in to the network as user SUPERVISOR       │
│ └───────────────────────────────────────────────────────────────┘   │
│ ┌───────────────────────────────────────────────────────────────┐   │
│ │                        Network Audit Log                        │   │
│ │                                                                 │   │
│ │ Tuesday  May 2, 1992  9:41:14 am SUPERVISOR                     │   │
│ │     Server1 activated                                           │   │
│ │                                                                 │   │
│ │ Tuesday  May 2, 1992 10:52:28 am SUPERVISOR                     │   │
│ │     Server2 activated                                           │   │
│ │                                                                 │   │
│ │ Tuesday  June 2, 1992 8:18:54 am SUPERVISOR                     │   │
│ │     Installed MS Windows on Server1                             │   │
│ │                                                                 │   │
│ │ Tuesday  June 2, 1992 10:43:37 am SUPERVISOR                    │   │
│ │     Installed Laser printer on Server2                          │   │
│ │                                                                 │   │
│ │                                                                 │   │
│ │                                                                 │   │
│ └───────────────────────────────────────────────────────────────┘   │
│ F1-help  Esc-go back  ↑↓                                             │
└─────────────────────────────────────────────────────────────────────┘
```

Contents of the audit log

      If the log file is empty, a message, informing you of this, appears on the screen. You will then automatically return to the *Audit Log* menu.

5.   As soon as you press ⎡Esc⎤ to exit the display of the log file, a prompt appears on the screen, asking you whether you want to delete the contents of the file. Answer Yes only if you are certain that you won't need any more information from the contents of this file.

      To ensure that this log file doesn't grow too large, it should be deleted from time to time.

6.   Then you return to the *Audit log* menu. You can exit NET from here by pressing ⎡Alt⎤ ⎡F10⎤ and answering the *Exit Net* prompt with "Yes".

Now you know how to display the contents of a NetWare Lite audit log. In the next section we'll show you how to permanently save the contents of an audit log to another file.

Displaying the audit log

Necessary steps

```
NET Enter
Supervise the network Enter
Audit log Enter
Display audit log Enter
View contents of audit log
Press Esc
Answer Delete Log Contents with Yes or No
Press Alt F10 to exit
Answer exit prompt with Yes
```

9.4   Saving the Audit Log

In the last section you learned how to display the contents of the audit log on the screen. Now you're going to learn how to save the contents of the audit log to a separate file that you can edit.

When the contents of an audit log are saved to a separate (external) file, the data is always saved in a text (ASCII) format.

The following steps are necessary to save an audit log to a file:

1. Call the NET utility program from the DOS prompt with:

    NET Enter

2. Select *Supervise the network* in the main menu and press Enter.

3. Select *Audit log,* from the *Supervise the Network* menu, and press Enter.

4. In the submenu that follows, select *Save to a file;* you will then see a screen display similar to the following:

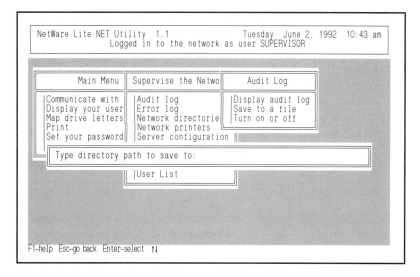

Saving the contents of the audit log

5.　Specify the name of the drive and directory in which you want to place the audit log. For example, you could specify a directory named C:\NWLITE. It's not necessary to specify the filename; NetWare Lite will save the audit log to a file named AUDIT.LOG as a default.

　Remember that the directory you specify (e.g., \NWLITE) must already exist.

The contents of the audit log are saved to a file called AUDIT.LOG.

6.　After you press Enter to confirm the directory name you entered, the file is saved in this directory. After a short time, a message informing you that the file has been saved, will appear on the screen.

Next, a prompt appears on the screen, asking whether you want to delete the audit log:

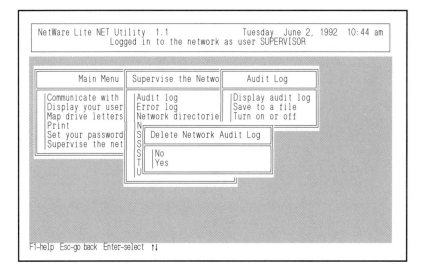

Deleting the audit log

   The deletion affects the current NetWare Lite audit
       log. The file you just saved will not be deleted.

7.   After you answer the prompt, you return to the *Audit log*
       menu. You can exit NET by pressing ⟦Alt⟧ ⟦F10⟧ and answering
       the *Exit NET* prompt with "Yes".

You have just learned how to save the audit log of the system to a
file. You can edit this file (AUDIT.LOG) since the data is in a text
(ASCII) format.

Saving the audit log

Necessary steps

```
NET ⟦Enter⟧
Supervise the network ⟦Enter⟧
Audit log ⟦Enter⟧
Save to a file ⟦Enter⟧
Enter the desired directory name
Confirm by pressing ⟦Enter⟧
Answer security prompt with Yes or No
Press ⟦Alt⟧ ⟦F10⟧ to exit
Answer exit prompt with Yes
```

9.5 Enabling/Disabling the Audit Log

The NET AUDIT command can be used to write entries to the audit log. This command can be entered at the DOS prompt to record changes made to the network, or placed within batch files to track a users activity. Please see Chapter 13 for more information on using the NET AUDIT command.

If you don't need to record user activities in an audit log, NetWare Lite gives you an option to suppress recording.

The following steps are necessary to suppress recording of user activities:

1.   First call the NET utility program from the DOS prompt with:

   NET [Enter]

2.   Select *Supervise the network* option from the main menu and press [Enter].

3.   Then select *Audit log* from the submenu that follows and confirm your selection by pressing [Enter].

4.   The *Audit Log* menu appears, in which you must select the *Turn on or off* option. A menu allowing you to turn the auditing on or off will appear as shown in the following figure:

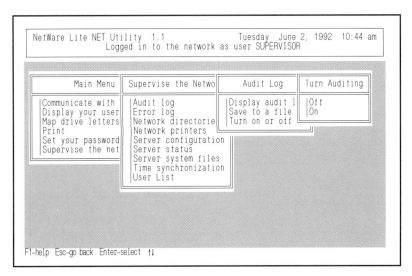

Turning off recording

5.   To suppress recording of user activities, choose *Off*.

      To turn recording back on, select *On*. The screen briefly displays a message informing you that recording has been turned off. Then you return to the *Audit log* menu.

6.   You can make further settings here or exit NET by pressing [Alt] [F10] and answering the *Exit NET* prompt with "Yes".

Now you know how to turn on/off the recording of user activities for the audit log.

      You cannot turn off recording of the error log of the network (ERROR.LOG).

Enabling/Disabling the audit log

Necessary steps

```
NET [Enter]
Supervise the network [Enter]
Audit log [Enter]
Turn on or off [Enter]
Select the desired option
Confirm by pressing [Enter]
Press [Alt] [F10] to exit
Answer exit prompt with Yes
```

9.6   Reconfiguring the Server

There are a number of system settings that influence the way the entire network runs when you use NetWare Lite. For example, you can set the maximum number of network printers or directories or define the maximum number of possible connections within a network. Monitoring and, if necessary, changing these settings are also duties of the supervisor. The following sections give you a detailed description of the most important of these tasks.

9.6.1   Changing the number of connections

In NetWare Lite you can connect a maximum of 25 computers to each other in a network. The default setting, which is entered during installation, amounts to four possible connections.

Here are the steps necessary for changing the maximum number of possible connections:

1.   Call the NET utility from the DOS prompt, with:

      NET (Enter)

2.   Select the *Supervise the network* option from the NET main menu and press (Enter).

3.   Then select *Server configuration* from the submenu that appears and confirm your choice by pressing (Enter).

      A list of the servers that are currently active will appear as shown in the following figure:

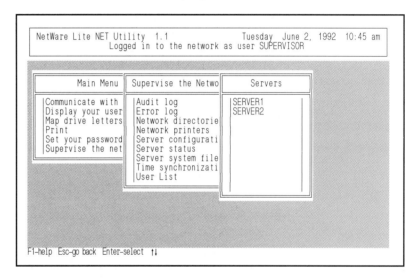

```
NetWare Lite NET Utility  1.1                 Tuesday  June 2, 1992  10:45 am
                      Logged in to the network as user SUPERVISOR

      Main Menu  │ Supervise the Netwo │    Servers

  Communicate with │ Audit log          │ SERVER1
  Display your user│ Error log          │ SERVER2
  Map drive letters│ Network directorie │
  Print            │ Network printers   │
  Set your password│ Server configurati │
  Supervise the net│ Server status      │
                   │ Server system file │
                   │ Time synchronizati │
                   │ User List          │


 F1-help  Esc-go back  Enter-select  ↑↓
```

Display of available servers

4.   Now select the name of the server for which you want to change the maximum number of possible connections.

      After pressing (Enter) to confirm your selection, another window appears, as shown in the following figure:

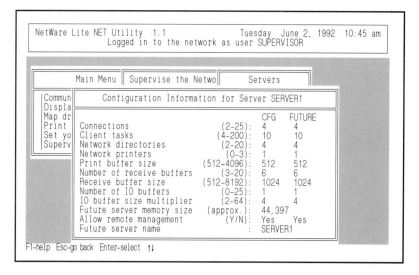

```
NetWare Lite NET Utility  1.1                    Tuesday  June 2, 1992  10:45 am
                    Logged in to the network as user SUPERVISOR

   ┌─────────────┬──────────────────┬──────────────┐
   │ Main Menu ║ Supervise the Netwo ║   Servers    │
   ┌─────────────────────────────────────────────┐
   │Commun ┌──────────────────────────────────────────┐
   │Displa │      Configuration Information for Server SERVER1
   │Map dr │                                    CFG    FUTURE
   │Print  │ Connections              (2-25):    4      4
   │Set yo │ Client tasks            (4-200):   10     10
   │Superv │ Network directories      (2-20):    4      4
          │ Network printers          (0-3):    1      1
          │ Print buffer size    (512-4096):  512    512
          │ Number of receive buffers (3-20):   6      6
          │ Receive buffer size (512-8192): 1024   1024
          │ Number of IO buffers     (0-25):    1      1
          │ IO buffer size multiplier (2-64):   4      4
          │ Future server memory size (approx.): 44,397
          │ Allow remote management   (Y/N):  Yes    Yes
          │ Future server name          :  SERVER1

 F1-help  Esc-go back  Enter-select  ↑↓
```

Server configuration

5.   Since the *Connections* option in the *FUTURE* column is
     already selected, you can now enter the desired number of
     connections. As soon as you type in a number, the old number
     will be overwritten. You can only enter a value between 2
     and 25. Then press Enter to confirm your selection.

     If you exit the program at this time by pressing Alt
     F10, all the changes you have made will be lost.

6.   Next, press Esc. A security prompt appears asking whether
     you want to save the changes.

7.   After answering Yes, you return to the list of available
     servers.

8.   Now you can make further settings or exit NET by pressing
     Alt F10 and answering the *Exit NET* prompt with "Yes".

You have just changed the maximum number of possible
connections. Remember that these changes don't go into effect until
the next time you reboot the server.

9.6.2   Changing the maximum number of network directories

The maximum number of possible network directories that can be
managed on a server is also limited. There can be from two to 20
different directories.

In Chapter 3 of this book you will find the necessary
explanations for setting up a network directory.
Chapter 4 explains how to access such a directory from
a workstation (client).

Here's how to set or change the maximum value of network
directories:

1.   Call the NET utility from the DOS prompt with:

      NET (Enter)

2.   Select the *Supervise the network* option from the main menu
      of NET and press (Enter).

3.   Next, select *Server configuration* from the *Supervise the
      Network* menu.

4.   A list of available servers appears. Select the name of the
      server for which you want to change the maximum number of
      possible network directories.

5.   After pressing (Enter) to confirm your choice, a window,
      showing the configuration options for the server, appears.
      Select the *Network directories* option in this window:

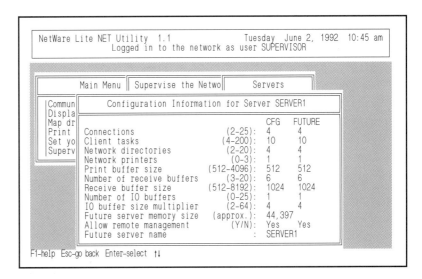

Server configuration

6.   Now you can enter the desired number and press (Enter). When
      you enter a number, the old entry is automatically
      overwritten. You may enter a value between 2 and 20.

☞   If you exit the program at this time by pressing [Alt] [F10], all the changes you have made will be lost.

7.   Next, press [Esc]. A security prompt appears asking whether you want to save the changes.

8.   After answering the prompt with "Yes", you return to the list of available servers.

9.   Now you can make further settings or exit NET by pressing [Alt] [F10] and answering the security prompt with "Yes".

You have just changed the number of maximum possible network directories that can be set up on the selected server. This change doesn't go into effect until you reboot the server.

9.6.3   Changing the number of network printers

You can also change the maximum number of network printers that can be set up on the server.

Here are the steps for changing the maximum number of network printers:

1.   Call the NET utility from the DOS prompt with:

      NET [Enter]

2.   Select the *Supervise the network* option from the main menu of NET and press [Enter].

3.   Next, select *Server configuration* from the *Supervise the Network* menu.

4.   A list of available servers appears. Select the name of the server for which you want to change the maximum number of possible network printers and press [Enter].

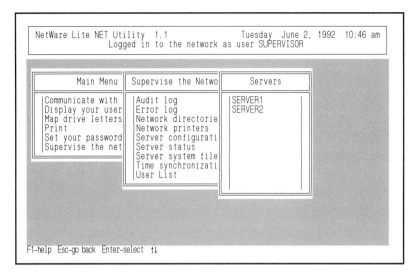

Display of available servers

5.   An additional window appears, showing the configuration
      information of the selected server. Use the cursor keys to
      select the *network printers* option:

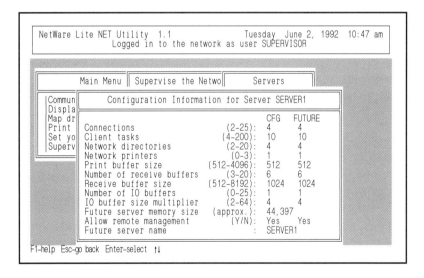

Server configuration

6.   Now you can enter the desired number of network printers
      and press (Enter) to confirm the change. As soon as you enter a
      number here, the old number is overwritten. You can only
      enter values from 0 to 3.

If you exit the program at this time by pressing [Alt]
[F10], all the changes you have made will be lost.

7.   Next, press [Esc]. A security prompt appears asking whether
      you want to save the changes.

8.   After answering "Yes", you return to the list of available
      servers.

9.   Now you can make further settings or exit NET by pressing
      [Alt] [F10] and answering the *Exit NET* prompt with "Yes".

You have just changed the maximum number of possible network
printers. Remember that this change doesn't go into effect until you
reboot the server.

9.6.4   Changing the server name

During installation, every server is assigned a name. This name
should be unique; otherwise there could be problems with using
NetWare Lite.

However, if you assigned the same name to two different servers,
you have an option of changing the name of a server:

1.   Call the NET utility from the DOS prompt with:

      NET [Enter]

2.   Select the *Supervise the network* option from the main menu
      of NET and press [Enter].

3.   Next, select *Server configuration* from the *Supervise the
      Network* menu.

4.   A list of available servers appears. Select the name of the
      server for which you want to change the name and press
      [Enter].

5.   An additional window appears showing the configuration
      options for the selected server. Use the cursor keys to select
      the *Future server name* option in this window and press
      [Enter]:

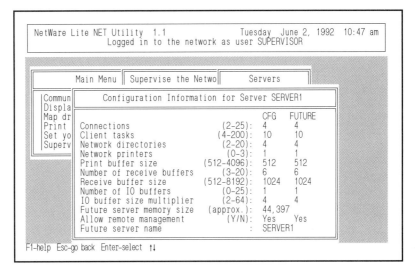

```
NetWare Lite NET Utility  1.1                Tuesday  June 2, 1992  10:47 am
                    Logged in to the network as user SUPERVISOR


        Main Menu ║ Supervise the Netwo ║      Servers
   Commun║       Configuration Information for Server SERVER1
   Displa║
   Map dr║                                        CFG    FUTURE
   Print ║ Connections               (2-25):     4      4
   Set yo║ Client tasks              (4-200):    10     10
   Superv║ Network directories       (2-20):     4      4
          Network printers          (0-3):      1      1
          Print buffer size      (512-4096):    512    512
          Number of receive buffers (3-20):     6      6
          Receive buffer size   (512-8192):     1024   1024
          Number of IO buffers      (0-25):     1      1
          IO buffer size multiplier (2-64):     4      4
          Future server memory size (approx.):  44,397
          Allow remote management   (Y/N):      Yes    Yes
          Future server name         :          SERVER1

 F1-help  Esc-go back  Enter-select  ↑↓
```

Server configuration

6. Next, use the ⌈Backspace⌉ key to delete the existing name.

7. Now you can enter a new name for the server.

☞   The name of a server can be up to 15 characters in
        length. Also, spaces are automatically replaced by an
        underscore, since a space is not considered a valid
        character in this context.

8. After you enter the new name, press ⌈Enter⌉ to confirm the new
    name.

☞   If you exit the program at this time by pressing ⌈Alt⌉
        ⌈F10⌉, all the changes you have made will be lost.

9. Now, press ⌈Esc⌉. A security prompt appears asking whether
    you want to save the changes.

10. After answering "Yes" to the prompt, you return to the list of
    available servers.

11. Now you can make further settings or exit NET by pressing
    ⌈Alt⌉ ⌈F10⌉ and answering the *Exit NET* prompt with "Yes".

You have just changed the name of the selected server. However,
this setting is not valid until the next time you reboot the server.

9.6.5 Increasing the tasks of the server

The activities of a server are generally specified in tasks. A task always refers to a certain activity. For example, copying a file from the server is a task.

The number of tasks that a server performs simultaneously is not infinite, but restricted by NetWare Lite. Here's how to change the maximum number of these tasks:

1.   Call the NET utility from the DOS prompt with:

      NET (Enter)

2.   Select the *Supervise the network* option from the main menu of NET and press (Enter).

3.   Next, select *Server configuration* from the *Supervise the Network* menu.

4.   A list of available servers appears. Select the name of the server for which you want to change the maximum number of tasks and press (Enter).

5.   A window appears showing the configuration information for the server. Use the cursor keys to select the *Client Tasks* option:

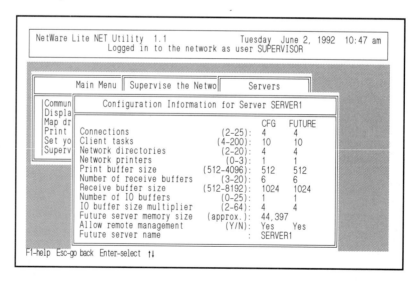

Server configuration

6.   Now you can enter the desired number of tasks and press (Enter). As soon as you enter a number here, the old entry is overwritten. You may enter a value between 4 and 200 here.

If you exit the program at this time by pressing (Alt) (F10), all the changes you have made will be lost.

7.   Next, press (Esc). A security prompt appears asking whether you want to save the changes.

8.   After answering "Yes", you return to the list of available servers.

9.   Now you can make further settings or exit NET by pressing (Alt) (F10) and answering the *Exit NET* prompt with "Yes".

You have just changed the maximum number of tasks performed simultaneously. This setting doesn't go into effect until you reboot the server.

9.6.6   Changing other configuration attributes

Along with changing the configuration attributes described in the previous sections, there are a number of other settings you can make. We'll discuss them briefly in this section.

These settings are also under the menu item *Server configuration*:

1.   First, select *Supervise the network* in the main menu of NET and press (Enter).

2.   Next, choose *Server configuration* from the submenu that appears and confirm by pressing (Enter). A list of the servers that are currently available appears.

3.   Select the name of the server from this list that you want to reconfigure:

        After you press (Enter) to confirm the name of the server, another window showing the configuration of the server appears, as shown in the following figure:

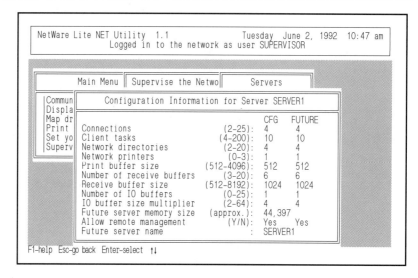

```
NetWare Lite NET Utility  1.1              Tuesday  June 2, 1992  10:47 am
                    Logged in to the network as user SUPERVISOR


       ┌──────────────┬──────────────────┬──────────────────┐
       │ Main Menu    │ Supervise the Netwo │   Servers       │
  ┌────┤              └──────────────────┴──────────────────┘
  │Commun│     Configuration Information for Server SERVER1
  │Displa│
  │Map dr│                                      CFG   FUTURE
  │Print │ Connections            (2-25):       4     4
  │Set yo│ Client tasks           (4-200):      10    10
  │Superv│ Network directories    (2-20):       4     4
  └──────┤ Network printers       (0-3):        1     1
         │ Print buffer size      (512-4096):   512   512
         │ Number of receive buffers (3-20):    6     6
         │ Receive buffer size    (512-8192):   1024  1024
         │ Number of IO buffers   (0-25):       1     1
         │ IO buffer size multiplier (2-64):    4     4
         │ Future server memory size (approx.): 44,397
         │ Allow remote management (Y/N):       Yes   Yes
         │ Future server name         :         SERVER1

 F1-help  Esc-go back  Enter-select  ↑↓
```

Server configuration

Different options for changing the server configuration appear in this window. We have already discussed some of these settings in the preceding sections.

Here are the settings available for reconfiguration:

Print buffer size

Use this setting to define an internal buffer for printer output. This setting applies to each network printer connected to the server.

Number of receive buffers

Use this setting to determine how many buffers are used to receive requests from the network users.

You can specify between 2 and 20 buffers.

Receive buffer size

Comparable to a print buffer, this setting is used to define a value for an area in which incoming requests to the server are stored.

Number of read buffers

This setting specifies the number of buffers available for the different read operations. You can enter values between 2 and 20 here.

Read buffer size

Use this setting to define the size of the read buffers on the server.

Allow remote management

To make changes to the server configuration from any workstation within the network, the supervisor must set *Allow remote management* to *Yes*. Then you can change all the settings of the *Configuration information* window at any workstation.

    To make changes to the server configuration, a user must have supervisor privileges (see also Chapter 6).

4.   After making the desired change, press (Esc) to exit the *Configuration information* window.

    If you exit the program at this time by pressing (Alt) (F10), all the changes you have made will be lost.

5.   After answering "Yes" to the security prompt, you return to the list of available servers.

6.   Now you can make further settings or exit NET by pressing (Alt) (F10) and answering the *Exit NET* prompt with "Yes".

You have just learned how to reconfigure a server.

    All changes that you make in the *Configuration information* window will go into effect after the server has been rebooted.

Reconfiguring a server

Necessary steps

NET (Enter)
Supervise the network (Enter)
Server configuration (Enter)
Select desired server and confirm by pressing (Enter)
Perform desired change
Confirm by pressing (Enter)
Press (Esc)
Answer security prompt with Yes
Press (Alt) (F10) to exit
Answer exit prompt with Yes

10.   Data Security And Backup

Data security is very important in network systems. One reason for this is the amount of users that work on network systems.

Network systems also handle larger volumes of data than stand-alone systems. So, a reliable method of data backup is also important. When data is lost on a network system, many users can be affected. Unless you back up your data, months or even years of work can be irretrievably lost in a moment. Because of this, it's especially important to perform daily data backups of the new data on your network system. You should also perform a complete backup frequently. By taking these precautions, you'll be able to restore most, if not all, of your data in case of a serious problem.

In this chapter we'll discuss the procedure used to backup the NetWare Lite system files. For example, these are the files that keep track of the network user names, network directories and network printers.

Only the NetWare Lite system information will be backed up and restored with the following procedure. All data on the network should be backed up separately at regular intervals. You may use the same procedure to backup the network data that you use to backup data on a stand-alone computer.

Also, when the system files are restored, the network will be configured as it was at the time of the backup. Any changes made after the NetWare Lite system files were last backed up will be lost.

10.1   Backing Up the System Files

Under NetWare Lite, the following procedure can be used to back up the system data maintained by the server. This should be done for each server on a regular basis:

1.   Start the NET utility program, by typing the following at the DOS prompt:

NET [Enter]

2.   From the main menu of NET, select the *Supervise the network* item and press Enter.

3.   Then select the *Server system files* option from the *Supervise the Network* menu and press Enter.

4.   A list of active servers will be displayed. Use the cursor keys to select the desired server and confirm your choice by pressing Enter.

5.   A menu listing the options (Back up and Restore) will be given. To backup the system files on the selected server, select the *Back up* option and press Enter.

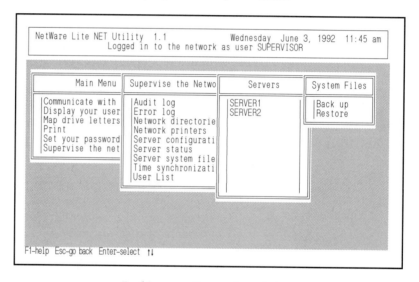

Backing up the system data

6.   You will be prompted to enter the drive and directory in which you would like the backup stored. Specify a name, such as C:\NWLITE, and press Enter. Do not enter a filename; a filename will be given by NetWare Lite.

          You must specify a directory that already exists on the server.

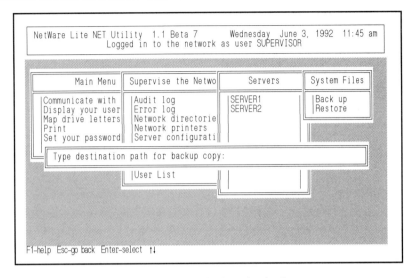

Entering the path for the backup

7. When completed you will be returned to the *System Files* menu. You can then continue working within NET or exit by pressing ⎡Alt⎦ ⎡F10⎦ and answering "Yes" at the *Exit NET* prompt that follows.

Backing up the NetWare Lite system files

Necessary steps

> NET ⎡Enter⎦
> Supervise the network ⎡Enter⎦
> Server system files ⎡Enter⎦
> Select the desired server and press ⎡Enter⎦
> Back up ⎡Enter⎦
> Enter desired path and press ⎡Enter⎦
> Press ⎡Alt⎦ ⎡F10⎦ to exit
> Answer exit prompt with Yes

10.2 Restoring the System Files

Under NetWare Lite, the following procedure can be used to restore a back up of the NetWare Lite system data:

1. Start the NET utility program by typing the following at the DOS prompt:

    NET ⎡Enter⎦

2. From the main menu of NET, select the *Supervise the network* item and press ⎡Enter⎦.

3. Then select the *Server system files* option from the *Supervise the Network* menu and press Enter.

4. A list of active servers will be displayed. Use the cursor keys to select the desired server and confirm your choice by pressing Enter.

5. A menu listing the options (Back up and Restore) will be given. To restore a backup of the system files on the selected server, select the *Restore* item and press Enter.

6. You will be prompted to enter the drive and directory in which the back up was stored. Specify the path that was given when you made the backup, such as C:\NWLITE, and press Enter.

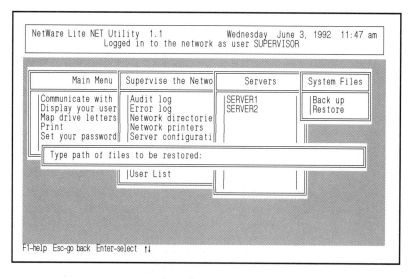

Restoring the system files

7. You will be prompted to back up the user file. If you have added users since the backup was made, and have not had any problems with the user names on the server, select "No". Otherwise, you should answer "Yes" at this prompt.

   A message will be given when the system has been successfully restored.

8. When completed you will be returned to the *System Files* menu. You can then continue working within NET or exit by pressing Alt F10 and answering "Yes" at the *Exit NET* prompt that follows.

Restoring the NetWare Lite system files

Necessary steps

NET [Enter]
Supervise the network [Enter]
Server system files [Enter]
Select the desired server and press [Enter]
Restore [Enter]
Enter desired path and press [Enter]
Press [Alt] [F10] to exit
Answer exit prompt with Yes

11.   The NetWare Lite Environment

In this chapter we'll present some tips for working within the NetWare Lite environment, such as synchronizing the date and time on the network servers or displaying information about the system.

11.1   Synchronizing the Date and Time

If you are working with applications or programming languages that use the file date and time information, you can synchronize the time and date on the network servers.

     Remote management must be enabled on each of the servers for which you would like to synchronize the date and time.

You can use the NET utility program to synchronize the time on the network servers as follows:

1.   Start the NET utility program from the DOS prompt, with the following:

       NET Enter

2.   Select the *Supervise the network* option from the main menu of NET and press Enter.

     If you are not familiar with operating NetWare Lite menus, it is described in Chapter 3 of this book.

       You can also get online help by pressing F1.

3.   From the *Supervise the Network* menu, select the *Time synchronization* item and press Enter. A screen similar to the following will appear:

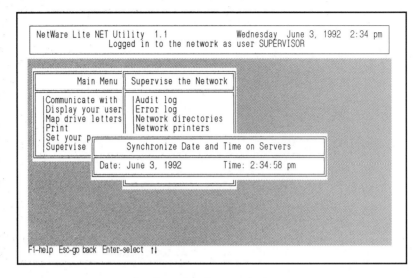

Setting the date and time

4.   You can use the cursor keys to select the date and time
      options. When you press (Enter) a text cursor will appear in
      the input line. You can use the (Backspace) key to delete the
      old entry and then type in the new settings.

5.   When the new date and time entries have been made, press
      (Esc) to exit, and answer "Yes" to the *Synchronize Date and
      Time on Servers* prompt.

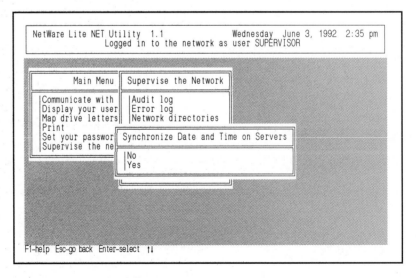

Synchronizing the date and time

6.   The date and time on the active file servers has now been
      synchronized. You may continue working within NET or exit

by pressing [Alt] [F10] and answering "Yes" to the *Exit NET* prompt.

Synchronizing the date and time

Necessary steps

```
NET [Enter]
Supervise the network [Enter]
Time synchronization [Enter]
Enter desired data and time
Press [Esc]
Answer synchronize data and time prompt with Yes
Press [Alt] [F10] to exit
Answer Yes to exit prompt
```

11.2   Which Version of NetWare Lite?

If you need to find out what version of NetWare Lite is installed, or what user name you are currently logged in under, you can use the NET INFO command.

Type the following command at the DOS prompt:

```
NET INFO [Enter]
```

The following information will be displayed:

```
Name of server...........SERVER1
Version of SERVER.EXE.... 1.1
Version of Client.EXE.....1.1
Your current username.....MIKE
Version of NET.EXE........1.1
Machine address..........00000002:00001B1D92AB
```

11.3   Information on the Logged in Users

The NET ULIST command will display a list of the network users currently logged in to the network. This can be very useful if you are sending messages through the network and need to find out who is logged in.

To display a list of the users that are currently logged in, type the following command at the DOS prompt:

```
NET ULIST [Enter]
```

A screen similar to the following will be displayed:

```
Connected Users          Address
===============          ============
```

```
*MIKE                    00001B1D92AB
SUPERVISOR               00001D3E16B8
JIM                      00001E451A3E

Total connected users: 3
```

The user names and node addresses of all users currently connected to the network will be displayed.

 An asterisk will appear next to the user name you are currently logged in under.

11.4   Displaying Server Information

The NET utility program can be used to display information on the file server's performance. The information provided can help you determine if the server configuration should be changed to improve the operation of the network.

Use the following procedure to view the file server's statistics:

1.   Start the NET utility from the DOS prompt, with the following command:

NET Enter

2.   Select the *Supervise the network* option from the main menu of NET and press Enter.

3.   From the *Supervise the Network* menu, select the *Server status* option and press Enter.

4.   A list of active servers will then be displayed. Use the cursor keys to selected the desired server and press Enter.

5.   Information on the selected server will then be displayed, as shown in the following figure.

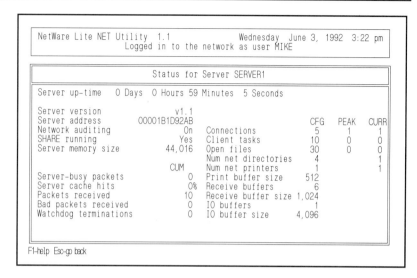

```
NetWare Lite NET Utility  1.1              Wednesday  June 3, 1992  3:22 pm
                     Logged in to the network as user MIKE

┌─────────────────────────────────────────────────────────────────────┐
│                       Status for Server SERVER1                       │
├─────────────────────────────────────────────────────────────────────┤
│ Server up-time    0 Days  0 Hours 59 Minutes  5 Seconds               │
│                                                                       │
│ Server version              v1.1                                      │
│ Server address        00001B1D92AB                       CFG PEAK CURR│
│ Network auditing              On   Connections            5    1    1  │
│ SHARE running                Yes   Client tasks          10    0    0  │
│ Server memory size        44,016   Open files            30    0    0  │
│                                    Num net directories    4         1  │
│                              CUM   Num net printers        1         1  │
│ Server-busy packets            0   Print buffer size    512            │
│ Server cache hits             0%   Receive buffers         6            │
│ Packets received              10   Receive buffer size 1,024           │
│ Bad packets received           0   IO buffers             1            │
│ Watchdog terminations          0   IO buffer size      4,096           │
│                                                                       │
└─────────────────────────────────────────────────────────────────────┘
 F1-help  Esc-go back
```

Status information for the server

The following information will be given in the server status screen:

Server version

Displays the current version number of the NetWare Lite SERVER.EXE program.

Server address

The node address of the selected file server.

Network auditing

Indicates whether or not network auditing has been enabled.

SHARE running

Indicates whether or not the DOS SHARE program has been activated on the selected server.

Server memory size

Displays the amount of memory reserved for the server (calculated using the number and size of the buffers).

Server-busy packets

The number of requests received that the server was too busy to handle.

Server cache hits

The number of file requests handled by the cache.

Packets received

Displays the number of packets received by the server.

Bad packets received

Displays the number of bad packets the server has received. A high number indicates that there may be a problem with the network hardware.

Watchdog terminations

If a network user shuts off the workstation without logging out, the server will clear the connection. The connections cleared by the server in this manner are called *watchdog terminations.*

Connections

This item shows information on the network connections. The maximum number of connections allowed by the server will be displayed, along with the peak number and current number of connections.

Client Tasks

Displays the number of tasks the server can handle at one time. The maximum number of tasks allowed by the server, the peak number and the current number of tasks will be displayed.

Open files

Displays information on the number of files that can be open at any given time. The maximum, peak and current numbers will be displayed.

Num net directories

Displays information on the number of network directories on the server. The maximum, peak and current number of network directories will be shown.

Num net printers

Displays information on the number of network printers. The maximum number of printers allowed by the server will be displayed, along with the peak number and current number of network printers.

Print buffer size

Indicates the size of the print buffer. A buffer is a given amount of memory reserved for temporary storage.

Receive buffers

The number of buffers that can be used by the server for workstation requests.

Receive buffer size

The size of each receive buffer.

Num IO buffers

The number of buffers that can be used by the server for read and write operations.

IO buffer size

The size of each of the IO buffers.

Checking the server's statistics

Necessary steps

```
NET Enter
Supervise the network Enter
Server status Enter
Select the desired server and press Enter
Press Alt F10 to exit
Answer Yes to exit prompt
```

11.5   Help with NetWare Lite Commands

The NET HELP command displays on-screen help for every NetWare Lite command. A description of the command and parameters will be given with an example.

To display a list of all NetWare Lite commands, type the following at the DOS prompt:

    NET HELP Enter

To display help on a specific NetWare Lite command, type the following at the DOS prompt:

NET HELP command [Enter]

In this example, "command" should be replaced with the command you would like help on. For example, to display help on the CAPTURE command, type the following:

NET HELP CAPTURE [Enter]

A screen similar to the following will be displayed, showing the syntax and a description of the command.

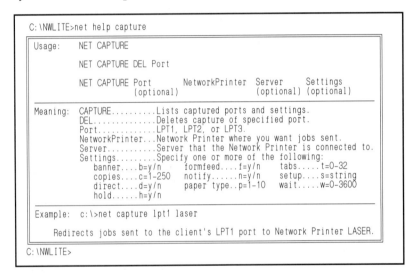

```
C:\NWLITE>net help capture

Usage:    NET CAPTURE

          NET CAPTURE DEL Port

          NET CAPTURE Port       NetworkPrinter  Server    Settings
                      (optional)                 (optional) (optional)

Meaning:  CAPTURE..........Lists captured ports and settings.
          DEL..............Deletes capture of specified port.
          Port.............LPT1, LPT2, or LPT3.
          NetworkPrinter...Network Printer where you want jobs sent.
          Server...........Server that the Network Printer is connected to.
          Settings.........Specify one or more of the following:
            banner....b=y/n    formfeed....f=y/n    tabs.....t=0-32
            copies....c=1-250  notify......n=y/n    setup....s=string
            direct....d=y/n    paper type..p=1-10   wait.....w=0-3600
            hold......h=y/n

Example:  c:\>net capture lpt1 laser

   Redirects jobs sent to the client's LPT1 port to Network Printer LASER.

C:\NWLITE>
```

  Chapter 13 lists all the NetWare Lite commands, with a description and examples, in alphabetical order.

11.6   Displaying Information on your Personal User Account

Use the following procedure to display information on your personal user account.

1.   Start the NET utility from the DOS prompt with:

      NET [Enter]

2.   Use the cursor keys to select the *Display your user account* menu item and press [Enter].

A screen similar to the following will appear showing information about your user account.

```
NetWare Lite NET Utility  1.1              Wednesday  June 3, 1992  2:36 pm
                      Logged in to the network as user MIKE


        ┌─────────────────────────┐
        │        Main Menu        │
        ├─────────────────────────┤
        │Communicate with users   │
        │Dis┌──────────────────────────────────────────────┐
        │Map│        Account Information for User MIKE       │
        │Pri├──────────────────────────────────────────────┤
        │Set│ User's full name         (25 max):            │
        │Sup│ Account disabled           (Y/N): No          │
        └───│ Supervisor privileges      (Y/N): Yes         │
            │ Password                      :               │
            │   Required                 (Y/N): No          │
            │   Minimum length          (1-15):             │
            │   Must be unique           (Y/N):             │
            │   Periodic changes required (Y/N):            │
            │   Days between changes   (1-100):             │
            │   Expiration date             :               │
            └──────────────────────────────────────────────┘

F1-help  Esc-go back
```

Display of account information

     The account information cannot be changed using this procedure. Chapter 5 will give a full description of each of these settings, with the steps necessary to make changes.

3.   When finished, you can either press (Esc) and continue to work within NET, or exit the program by pressing (Alt) (F10) and answering "Yes" to the *Exit NET* prompt that follows.

Displaying information on your account

Necessary steps

```
NET (Enter)
Display your user account (Enter)
Press (Alt) (F10) to exit
Answer Yes to the exit prompt
```

12.   Implementing Application Programs

A network system's power is revealed when application programs are implemented on the network. By doing this, you can, for example, create files with a database program and make the data available to all network users. Data created by any workstation can be accessed by the other workstations.

Although the procedures for installing and setting up application programs on a network system are similar to the procedures for stand-alone PCs, you should remember a few important points. In this chapter we'll present the information you'll need in order to use application programs on your network system.

12.1   Running Programs in a Network Environment

Basically any program that can run under MS-DOS on a stand-alone PC can be implemented on a network. However, problems can occur when two users working with the program try to access the same data simultaneously. So network software must have a mechanism that prevents two users from writing to the same file simultaneously. If this happens, the program wouldn't know which data to write to the file or which user should be given precedence.

This access problem only applies to the data generated with an application program. Since the application program's software is copied from the network drive to the workstation's memory, access problems don't occur when users run these programs. In order to run the application program, users simply make their own copies in their workstation's memory.

A program that has built-in precautions to prevent simultaneous write access to data is called a *network version*. There are two mechanisms for protecting network data from simultaneous access: *record locking*, which prevents two users from accessing the same record in a file, and *file locking*, which prevents two users from accessing the same file.

Before purchasing a program that you want to implement on your network, you should determine whether or not there is a network version of the program. This is extremely important since a *data collision*, which we previously described, is not only inconvenient but can also lead to data loss.

If the application that you are installing asks what type of network you are using, DO NOT choose "Novell" or "NetWare". You should choose "Peer-to-Peer", "Other" or "None".

12.2 Creating a Directory for a New Program

You should always create a new directory for all application programs that you install on your network. Remember that in order to avoid confusion, you should never copy application program software to the root directory. The best thing to do is create a separate directory (called APPS or some other suitable name), under the root directory, which contains subdirectories for each application program.

Use the MS-DOS command MD from the operating system level to create a new directory. For example:

```
MD C:\APPS\NEW_PRG [Enter]
```

 If the program you want to use has its own installation program, usually you don't have to create a directory for it yourself. Simply enter the desired directory name when prompted by the installation routine; the software will then be stored in this directory.

The command previously given will create a new subdirectory called NEW_PRG under the directory APPS. If the software doesn't include an installation routine, you'll have to copy the program files to the new directory. Insert the program diskette in drive A: and type the following operating system command:

```
COPY A:*.* C:\APPS\NEW_PRG [Enter]
```

All files on the diskette in drive A: will then be copied to the directory \APPS\NEW_PRG on drive C:.

12.3 Defining a Network Directory

As previously mentioned, one of the basic principles of NetWare Lite, sharing resources, is made possible by assigning names to the resources. The resources can then be accessed by the workstation, using these network names.

Before an application can be used on the network, a network directory should be defined so that the network users can access it. The following procedure can be used to define a network directory.

1. First, call the NET utilities program at the DOS prompt
    with:

        NET [Enter]

2. Then select the *Supervise the network* option from the main
    menu and press [Enter].

3. From this menu, select the item called *Network directories*.
    A window showing the available network directories will
    be displayed, as shown in the following figure. If you have
    just installed NetWare Lite, you will only see the default,
    CDRIVE.

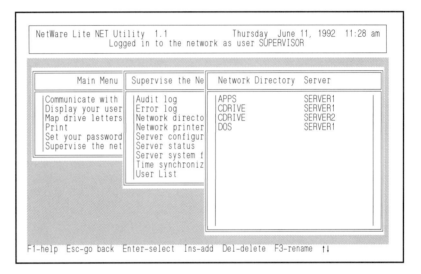

Display of the network directories

The CDRIVE is automatically assigned as a network
directory during installation. This name refers to the root
directory of hard drive C:, making it possible to access the
entire hard drive (including subdirectories).

This is a default which you can delete at any time. Simply
highlight this name and then press [Del]. If you answer Yes to
the *Delete Network Directory* prompt, the directory will be
removed from the list.

4. To define a new network directory, first press [Ins]. A list of
    the active servers in the network appears.

5. Select the name of the server for which you want to assign a
    network directory. After selecting the server, you will be
    prompted for the name of the network directory. The name

can use any combination of letters and numbers and be up to 15 characters in length. This is the name that will be used by the workstations (clients), so be sure to make it a meaningful name.

6.   Enter the name (e.g., APPS) and confirm it by pressing [Enter].

After entering the network directory name, you will be required to enter the actual name of the directory, including the path, and also assign the access rights users will have to this network directory.

7.   To do this, select the *Actual directory path* prompt and press [Enter]. You will then be given a cursor so that you can enter the actual directory name as it exists on the server (e.g., C:\APPS) and confirm it by pressing [Enter].

☞   If the directory is on a drive other than C:, you can use the [Backspace] key to delete C: and enter the new drive letter (e.g., D:\APPS).

After entering the actual directory name, you must define the access rights to the directory. Access rights define the type of access the network users will have to the files in this directory.

If you are unfamiliar with access rights, the next section gives a full description of the available access rights and the procedure used to define them. You should skip ahead to the next section at this time.

8.   After specifying the actual path to the network directory, you should assign the desired access rights.

9.   After assigning the access rights to the network directory, press [Esc] and answer "Yes" to the *Save changes* prompt.

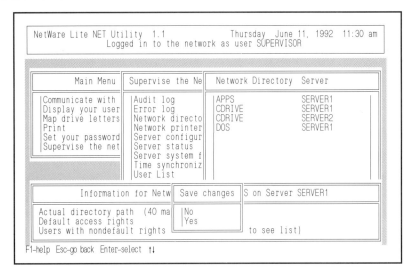

```
NetWare Lite NET Utility  1.1            Thursday  June 11, 1992  11:30 am
                  Logged in to the network as user SUPERVISOR


        Main Menu    Supervise the Ne  Network Directory  Server

   Communicate with  Audit log        APPS               SERVER1
   Display your user Error log         CDRIVE             SERVER1
   Map drive letters Network directo   CDRIVE             SERVER2
   Print             Network printer   DOS                SERVER1
   Set your password Server configur
   Supervise the net Server status
                     Server system f
                     Time synchroniz
                     User List

        Information for Netw  Save changes  S on Server SERVER1

   Actual directory path  (40 ma   No
   Default access rights             Yes
   Users with nondefault rights               to see list)

F1-help  Esc-go back  Enter-select  ↑↓
```

Saving the network directory information

10.   This completes the steps necessary to define a network
      directory. You may either continue to work within NET or
      exit by pressing Alt F10 and answering "Yes" to the *Exit NET*
      prompt.

12.4   Assigning Access Rights to a Network Directory

Defining access rights is another important factor in setting up
applications on the network. Without the necessary rights, it is
impossible for users to access the files in the network directories.

There are two different procedures for assigning access rights in
NetWare Lite. You can grant default access rights to a network
directory (for all users) or you can assign each user individual
access rights, called nondefault rights.

  The default access rights will apply to all users. If an
individual user requires different access rights,
nondefault access rights must be given to that user.

Access rights are used to define the kinds of access the individual
users within the network have to the files stored in a network
directory. For example, the supervisor can determine that users
may read certain files, but never make changes to them. In other
words, the users have read access but not write access.

NetWare Lite provides you with the following access rights when
you setup network directories:

ALL

Allows unrestricted access to the files of the specified directory. Users may read, delete, execute and make changes to files.

This is the highest priority level of access rights for network directories.

NONE

No access of any kind is permitted.

READ

Users may read files, but may not make changes to, or delete files.

The following steps will enable you to define or modify the access rights of a network directory:

1.   First call the NET utility program, using the following command:

     NET [Enter]

2.   Then select *Supervise the network* option in the main menu of NET.

    If you're unfamiliar with the operation of the NetWare Lite menus, read Chapter 3 of this book. You will find detailed information about operating this menu there.

     You can also call online help at any time by pressing [F1].

3.   Select the *Network directories* item from the *Supervise the network* menu. A list of the defined network directories appears, as shown in the following figure:

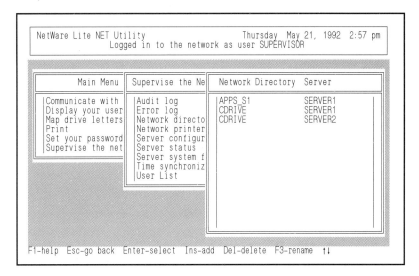

```
┌─────────────────────────────────────────────────────────────────┐
│ NetWare Lite NET Utility                   Thursday  May 21, 1992  2:57 pm │
│            Logged in to the network as user SUPERVISOR            │
│  ┌──────────────────────────────────────────────────────────┐  │
│  │  Main Menu    │ Supervise the Ne│ Network Directory  Server │  │
│  │ ┌───────────────┬────────────────┬─────────────────────────┐ │
│  │ │Communicate with│Audit log       │APPS_S1        SERVER1   │ │
│  │ │Display your user│Error log       │CDRIVE         SERVER1   │ │
│  │ │Map drive letters│Network directo │CDRIVE         SERVER2   │ │
│  │ │Print           │Network printer │                         │ │
│  │ │Set your password│Server configur │                         │ │
│  │ │Supervise the net│Server status   │                         │ │
│  │ │                │Server system f │                         │ │
│  │ │                │Time synchroniz │                         │ │
│  │ │                │User List       │                         │ │
│  │ └───────────────┴────────────────┴─────────────────────────┘ │
│ F1-help  Esc-go back  Enter-select  Ins-add  Del-delete  F3-rename  ↑↓ │
└─────────────────────────────────────────────────────────────────┘
```

Display of the available network directories

4. Use the cursor keys to select the name of the network directory whose default access rights you want to change.

5. After you confirm your choice of network directory by pressing Enter, a window appears with additional information on the selected directory:

6. In the *Default access rights* text box you will find the specification of default access rights. To change this setting, use the cursor keys to select this item and press Enter.

    A new window appears showing the access right options that are available:

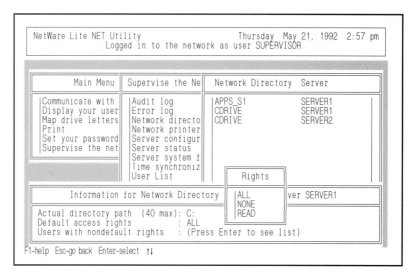

Selecting access rights

7.   Now select the option you want to assign as the default access right to the selected directory. Use the cursor keys to select it and press (Enter).

8.   The access right you selected then appears in the window after *Default access rights*.

      You can also assign nondefault access rights at this time, if necessary. This will allow you to "customize" the access rights granted to individual users. Let's suppose that you assigned READ to a network directory as a default access right. That means that all users can only read the files in this directory; none of the users will be able to edit the files.

      However, if you want to grant a certain user the right to make changes to the existing files, NetWare Lite has a solution. This solution consists of assigning individual users rights that differ from the default access rights for the network directory or nondefault access rights.

      The following steps describe how to grant nondefault access rights to a user.

9.   Select the *Users with nondefault rights* option in the window showing the network directory information.

10.   Now press (Enter) to see a list of users who already have nondefault rights for this network directory. If no one has been assigned nondefault rights for this network directory, the list will be empty.

11.   Next, press ⌈Ins⌉ to see a list of usernames that have been defined on the network.

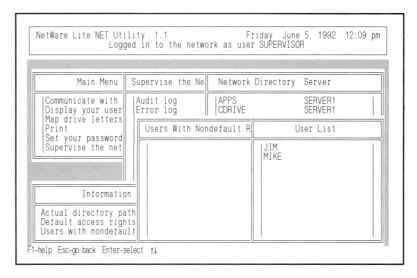

Display of the defined usernames

12.   Select the user whom you want to assign nondefault access rights.

13.   After you confirm your selection by pressing ⌈Enter⌉, another window appears, displaying the possible access rights.

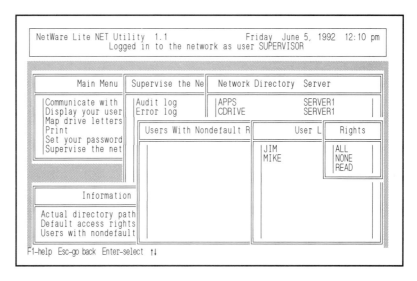

The nondefault access rights

14.   Select the access right you want to assign to the user as a nondefault right for the network directory.

15.   After you press (Enter), the selected username and assigned access right appear on the screen, as shown in the next figure:

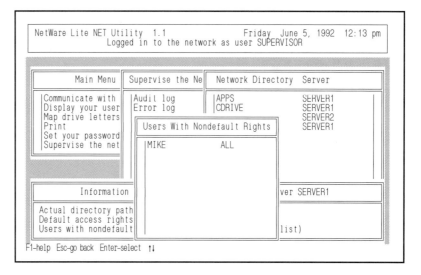

```
NetWare Lite NET Utility  1.1                      Friday  June 5, 1992  12:13 pm
                    Logged in to the network as user SUPERVISOR


          Main Menu    Supervise the Ne   Network Directory   Server
        Communicate with  Audit log        APPS              SERVER1
        Display your user  Error log        CDRIVE            SERVER1
        Map drive letters                                    SERVER2
        Print              Users With Nondefault Rights       SERVER1
        Set your password
        Supervise the net    MIKE            ALL


          Information                                       ver SERVER1
        Actual directory path
        Default access rights
        Users with nondefault                               list)
F1-help  Esc-go back  Enter-select  ↑↓
```

Username and assigned access right

    To assign nondefault access rights to other users for the selected directory, simply press (Ins) again and follow the same procedure.

16.   To exit the list of usernames with nondefault rights, press (Esc).

    Remember that if you exit NET at this time by pressing (Alt) (F10), all the changes you made will be lost.

17.   To save the settings, you must press (Esc) again, which returns you to the list of available network directories.

18.   Now you can make further settings or exit NET safely by pressing (Alt) (F10) and answering "Yes" to the *Exit NET* prompt.

The new access rights you assigned will be valid the next time the user logs in to the network.

12.5 Protecting a New Program From Accidental Deletion

While the SHARE program will help to protect against data collision, it will not guard against the accidental deletion of files on the network. You can, however, set the READ-ONLY attribute to protect the network programs from changes or accidental deletions.

Before a READ-ONLY file can be deleted, the READ-ONLY attribute must be removed. This extra step decreases the chances that a READ-ONLY file will be accidentally deleted.

The following command can be used to set the READ-ONLY attribute on a file:

```
ATTRIB +R path\filename Enter
```

For example, to set the READ-ONLY attribute on the C:\APPS\TEXT.EXE file, you would use the following command:

```
ATTRIB +R C:\APPS\TEXT.EXE Enter
```

You can also use wildcards with this command. To set the READ-ONLY attribute on all .EXE files in C:\APPS, you would use the following command:

```
ATTRIB +R C:\APPS\*.EXE Enter
```

12.6 Implementing WordPerfect on the Network

As an example of the extra steps used when installing applications on a NetWare Lite network, this section contains information on the network implementation of WordPerfect 5.1. Use the following steps to install WordPerfect on the network drive:

1. Run the WordPerfect installation program on the Install/Learn/Utilities 1 diskette by typing the following at the DOS prompt:

    ```
    A:INSTALL Enter
    ```

2. Press Y to continue with the installation.

3. Press Y to install to a hard disk.

4. From the Installation screen, select option 3 for Network Installation.

5.   If you need to change the *Install From* drive, press ① and type in the proper drive at the *Install From:* prompt.

6.   You should change the *Install To* directory to a directory on the network drive, such as APPS\WP51. Press ② to select this option and enter the full directory name. If the directory doesn't exist, press Ⓨ when asked if you would like to create the directory. The other directory options listed should change to this new entry automatically. You can then press Ⓔsc to return to the previous menu.

7.   Press ③ to *Install Disks*. You will be given a number of installation options at this point. You should install whatever you may need to use on your network in the future. The program will ask whether or not you would like to install each option separately and request the diskettes as they are needed.

8.   Choose option 4 to check the CONFIG.SYS and AUTOEXEC.BAT files. Press Ⓝ when asked if you would like to add WordPerfect to your path.

9.   Press ⑤ to Check WP{WP}.ENV. If this file doesn't exist, the program will ask if you would like to create it. To do this press Ⓨ. The subsequent screen will list a number of network options; press Ⓞ to select the *Other* option.

10.   You'll then be asked to enter a directory name for the Setup files. All WordPerfect users must have ALL rights in this directory in order to create and modify their starting environment. For security reasons, we recommend you use a shared directory that is separate from the program files, such as APPS\WP51\SETUP. If this directory doesn't exist, press Ⓨ to create it.

11.   After returning to the main menu you should either Exit or Install Printers and Exit.

      Network printers can be installed from within WordPerfect by using the same procedure that is used for a local printer.

12.   After returning to DOS, set up the WordPerfect directory as a network directory and make the program files read-only. You must also grant ALL access rights to the SETUP directory, so that the users can set up their own working environment.

13.   WordPerfect can be started with:

WP (Enter)

    When WordPerfect is started on a network, the user will be asked to enter 3 initials. These initials determine which configuration file is used when the program is loaded. Ensure that these initials are used consistently for each user/workstation and aren't duplicated.

13.   NetWare Lite Commands

This chapter contains an overview of all the NetWare Lite operating system commands. The command syntax and a description of how each command is used, will be given.

The following words are used in the command syntax descriptions. They'll be printed in small letters to distinguish them from the command words:

Term	Description
character	Any character string (text)
command	Name of a NetWare command
date	Date in the format MM-DD-YY
dir	Name of a directory including file server and volume
drive	Letter indicating a drive
file	Name of a file
fs	Name of a file server
job	Name of a print job
nlm	Name of a NetWare Loadable Module
number	A natural number
para	Additional parameters or options
path	A directory path name
proto	Name of a communication protocol
ps	Name of a print server
que	Name of a print queue
rights	Access rights or file attributes
search	A search drive
time	Time in the format HH:MM:SS
user	Name of a user or user group
volume	Name of a volume

In the syntax descriptions optional information will be enclosed in square brackets. This information doesn't have to be entered in order for the command to run. The following is a summary of all NetWare commands:

       The keyword NET must precede all Netware Lite commands on the command line. For example, when using the LOGIN command you must type the following:

NET LOGIN (Enter)

NET AUDIT

Syntax: NET AUDIT "log entry"

Function: The AUDIT command allows you to keep a log of the
              activity on the network. It is most often used from
              within batch files to keep track of the network users
              activity, but can also be issued from the command line
              to record any changes made to the network.

Notes: The log entry must be enclosed within quotation marks,
              and must be less than 80 characters in length.

              Also, the network supervisor must enable the use of the
              Audit Log before it can be used. Please see Section 9.5
              for more information on turning the audit log on and
              off.

Example: If you would like to record the installation of
              application programs on the network, use a command
              similar to the following to record it in the audit log:

              NET AUDIT "Installed myapp, 5/1/92"

NET CAPTURE

Syntax: NET CAPTURE

Syntax: NET CAPTURE port printer [server]
             [options]

Syntax: NET CAPTURE DEL port

Options: Banner   b=Y, b=N   (default Y)
             Copies   c= 1-250   (default 1)
             Direct=Y, b=N (default N)
             Formfeed   f=Y, f=N   (default Y)
             Papertype   p= 1-10   (default 1)
             Tabs   t= 0-32   (default 0)
             Wait   w= 0-3600   (default 10)
             Setup   s= printer
                            command

Example: To display the current capture settings, type the
              following at the DOS prompt:

              NET CAPTURE

Example: To capture the LPT1 port to the network printer named LASER on server SERVER1, use the capture command as follows:

        NET CAPTURE LPT1 LASER SERVER1

Example: To remove the capture of the LPT2 port, use the following command:

        NET CAPTURE DEL LPT2

NET HELP

Syntax: NET HELP [command]

Function: Displays help for the NetWare Lite commands.

Example: To display help on the NetWare Lite CAPTURE command, type the following:

        NET HELP CAPTURE

        To display a list of available help, use the following:

        NET HELP

NET INFO

Syntax: NET INFO

Function: Displays information about the network, including the versions of the NetWare Lite software and your username.

NET LOGIN

Syntax: NET LOGIN [username]

Function: Allows you to log in to the network. You will be prompted for the password, if one has been setup for your account.

Example: If your username is MIKE, the following command will log you in to the network.

        LOGIN MIKE

NET LOGOUT

Syntax: NET LOGOUT

Function: Logs you out of the network.

Example: Type the following command to log off the NetWare Lite network:

        NET LOGOUT

NET MAP

Syntax: NET MAP

Syntax: NET MAP driveletter: networkdirectory [server]

Syntax: NET MAP DEL driveletter:

Syntax: NET MAP NEXT networkdirectory [server]

Function: Used to display, setup and remove NetWare Lite drive mappings.

Example: Use the following command to display the current drive mappings:

        NET MAP

Example: To map drive letter H: to the network directory APPS on server SERVER1, use the following command:

        NET MAP H: APPS SERVER1

Example: To remove the network drive H:, use the following:

        NET MAP DEL H:

Example: The following command can be used to assign the next available drive letter to the network directory APPS:

        NET MAP NEXT APPS

NET NDLIST

Syntax: NET NDLIST

Function: Displays a list of the NetWare Lite network directories.

NET NPLIST

Syntax: NET NPLIST

Function: Displays a list of the NetWare Lite network printers.

NET PRINT

Syntax: NET PRINT filename [network printer]

Function: Prints a file to a network printer.

Notes: Before using this command you must use the CAPTURE command to set up a network printer. Also, if a printer is not specified when calling the command, the file will be sent to the printer attached to the first captured port.

Example: If the CAPTURE command was used to redirect output from LPT2: to a laser printer named LASER, you could use the NET PRINT command to print the README.TXT file on a diskette in drive A:

    NET PRINT A:\README.TXT LASER

If both LPT1: and LPT2: are captured, the following command would send the output of the README.TXT to LPT1:

    NET PRINT A:\README.TXT

NET RECEIVE

Syntax: NET RECEIVE ON|OFF

Function: Enables or suppresses the reception of messages on the workstation.

Example: The following command will suppress the reception of messages on the workstation:

```
NET RECEIVE OFF
```

To re-enable the reception of messages, use the following:

```
NET RECEIVE ON
```

NET SEND

Syntax: `NET SEND "message" username [username] [username]`

Syntax: `NET SEND ALL`

Notes: The message must be enclosed within quotation marks, and must be less than 30 characters in length.

Function: SEND allows you to send messages to other users that are logged in to the network.

Example: The following command sends a reminder of a sales meeting to Mike and Sheri:

```
SEND "Sales meeting at 1:00" Mike Sheri
```

You can also replace username with ALL to send the message to all users currently logged in to the network. For example:

```
SEND "The network will be shut down in 10 minutes" ALL
```

NET SETPASS

Syntax: `NET SETPASS`

Notes: A password cannot exceed 15 characters in length and must meet any other requirements (i.e., minimum length, unique passwords) set by the network supervisor.

Function: Allows you to set or change your password.

Example: The following command will allow you to change your password.

```
NET SETPASS
```

You will be prompted for your current password and then the new one. You will also be asked to retype the new password to verify it.

NET SLIST

Syntax: NET SLIST

Function: Displays a list of the NetWare Lite file servers that are available.

NET TIME

Syntax: NET TIME [server]

Notes: If a server is not specified, the time will be set with that of either the server, to which your default drive is mapped, or to the first server that responds to the request.

Function: Sets the workstations time, equal to that of the specified server.

NET ULIST

Syntax: NET ULIST

Function: ULIST displays a list of all users that are currently logged in to the network. NW_CLIENT will be listed to workstations that have loaded CLIENT, but not logged in yet.

Example: If you need to send Mike a message, you can use ULIST to check whether or not he is logged in to the network. Use ULIST as follows:

              NET ULIST

Appendix A: Keyboard Assignments

Keys used in book	Keys on other computers	Key
\<Alt\>	ALT	Alt
\<End\>	END	1 End or End
\<Home\>	HOME	7 Home or Home
\<Ctrl\>	CTRL, CONT	Ctrl
\<Del\>	DEL, DELETE	. Del or Delete
\<Ins\>	INS, INSERT	0 Ins or Insert
\<Enter\>	RETURN, ENTER	← Enter
\<Esc\>	Escape, ESCAPE, ESC	Esc
\<Backspace\>	BACK	← or ← Backspace
\<Shift\>	Shift, SHIFT	⇧ or ⇧ Shift
\<Tab\>	TAB	⇥ or ⇥ Tab
\<Pg Up\>	Page Up	9 PgUp or Page Up
\<Pg Dn\>	Page Down	3 PgDn or Page Down

Appendix B: ASCII Table

Dec	Hex	Char	Dec	Hex	Char	Dec	Hex	Char	Dec	Hex	Char
0	00		32	20		64	40	@	96	60	`
1	01	☺	33	21	!	65	41	A	97	61	a
2	02	☻	34	22	"	66	42	B	98	62	b
3	03	♥	35	23	#	67	43	C	99	63	c
4	04	♦	36	24	$	68	44	D	100	64	d
5	05	♣	37	25	%	69	45	E	101	65	e
6	06	♠	38	26	&	70	46	F	102	66	f
7	07	•	39	27	'	71	47	G	103	67	g
8	08	◘	40	28	(	72	48	H	104	68	h
9	09	o	41	29	)	73	49	I	105	69	i
10	0A	■	42	2A	*	74	4A	J	106	6A	j
11	0B	♂	43	2B	+	75	4B	K	107	6B	k
12	0C	♀	44	2C	,	76	4C	L	108	6C	l
13	0D	♪	45	2D	–	77	4D	M	109	6D	m
14	0E	♫	46	2E	.	78	4E	N	110	6E	n
15	0F	☼	47	2F	/	79	4F	O	111	6F	o
16	10	►	48	30	0	80	50	P	112	70	p
17	11	◄	49	31	1	81	51	Q	113	71	q
18	12	↕	50	32	2	82	52	R	114	72	r
19	13	‼	51	33	3	83	53	S	115	73	s
20	14	¶	52	34	4	84	54	T	116	74	t
21	15	§	53	35	5	85	55	U	117	75	u
22	16	▬	54	36	6	86	56	V	118	76	v
23	17	↨	55	37	7	87	57	W	119	77	w
24	18	↑	56	38	8	88	58	X	120	78	x
25	19	↓	57	39	9	89	59	Y	121	79	y
26	1A	→	58	3A	:	90	5A	Z	122	7A	z
27	1B	←	59	3B	;	91	5B	[	123	7B	{
28	1C	∟	60	3C	<	92	5C	\	124	7C		
29	1D	↔	61	3D	=	93	5D	]	125	7D	}
30	1E	▲	62	3E	>	94	5E	^	126	7E	~
31	1F	▼	63	3F	?	95	5F	_	127	7F	Δ

Dec	Hex	Char	Dec	Hex	Char	Dec	Hex	Char	Dec	Hex	Char
128	80	Ç	160	A0	á	192	C0	└	224	E0	α
129	81	ü	161	A1	í	193	C1	┴	225	E1	β
130	82	é	162	A2	ó	194	C2	┬	226	E2	Γ
131	83	â	163	A3	ú	195	C3	├	227	E3	π
132	84	ä	164	A4	ñ	196	C4	─	228	E4	Σ
133	85	à	165	A5	Ñ	197	C5	┼	229	E5	σ
134	86	å	166	A6	ª	198	C6	╞	230	E6	μ
135	87	ç	167	A7	º	199	C7	╟	231	E7	τ
136	88	ê	168	A8	¿	200	C8	╚	232	E8	Φ
137	89	ë	169	A9	⌐	201	C9	╔	233	E9	Θ
138	8A	è	170	AA	¬	202	CA	╩	234	EA	Ω
139	8B	ï	171	AB	½	203	CB	╦	235	EB	δ
140	8C	î	172	AC	¼	204	CC	╠	236	EC	∞
141	8D	ì	173	AD	¡	205	CD	═	237	ED	Ø
142	8E	Ä	174	AE	«	206	CE	╬	238	EE	∈
143	8F	Å	175	AF	»	207	CF	╧	239	EF	∩
144	90	É	176	B0	░	208	D0	╨	240	F0	≡
145	91	æ	177	B1	▒	209	D1	╤	241	F1	±
146	92	Æ	178	B2	▓	210	D2	╥	242	F2	≥
147	93	ô	179	B3	│	211	D3	╙	243	F3	≤
148	94	ö	180	B4	┤	212	D4	╘	244	F4	⌠
149	95	ò	181	B5	╡	213	D5	╒	245	F5	⌡
150	96	û	182	B6	╢	214	D6	╓	246	F6	÷
151	97	ù	183	B7	╖	215	D7	╫	247	F7	≈
152	98	ÿ	184	B8	╕	216	D8	╪	248	F8	°
153	99	Ö	185	B9	╣	217	D9	┘	249	F9	•
154	9A	Ü	186	BA	║	218	DA	┌	250	FA	·
155	9B	¢	187	BB	╗	219	DB	█	251	FB	√
156	9C	£	188	BC	╝	220	DC	▄	252	FC	ⁿ
157	9D	¥	189	BD	╜	221	DD	▌	253	FD	²
158	9E	₧	190	BE	╛	222	DE	▐	254	FE	■
159	9F	ƒ	191	BF	┐	223	DF	▀	255	FF	

Appendix C: Glossary

This appendix contains definitions of the most important and frequently used NetWare terms.

Access Rights   The network manager can assign access rights to limit a users access to files and directories on the network. Each user can be assigned different rights to any data on the network.

Accounting   The act of tracking file accesses and use of network resources.

ARCnet   One of the earliest and most popular local area networks invented. Abbreviation for Attached Resource Computer Network.

Baud Rate   Measurement of data transmission speed, measured in bits per second or bps.

Bindery   The bindery contains information on all objects defined in the network system. This includes user names and user groups (along with passwords), information on file servers, print servers, and print queues. Basically, any network object that has a name is listed in the bindery.

Boot   Booting your computer or network system means switching it on and activating the operating system.

Boot Diskette   A boot diskette (or start diskette) is the diskette used to boot a computer. Under NetWare, the file server and each workstation (except for diskless workstations) must have a boot diskette. The boot diskette must be inserted in the disk drive each time the computer is switched on so that the operating system files can be loaded and activated.

Bridge   Novell defines a connection between two network systems as a bridge. The second network can be of the same type or a different type. There are two types of bridges: internal and external. When two or more networks are installed on the same file server (using different network adapters), this is an internal bridge.

An external bridge is installed in a separate file server. This takes some of the processing load off the file server. A bridge can be installed as either a dedicated or non-dedicated bridge.

Bus   A network topology in which a single line or cable is shared by all workstations.

Cache Buffer   A cache buffer is part of the file server's memory that temporarily stores data from files that are being accessed. This enables the data to be accessed faster than if it were read directly from the hard disk.

Console Mode   In addition to the operating system mode, NetWare 286 and 386 can also be operated from the console mode. All NetWare console commands must be entered in console mode and a dedicated file server can only be operated in console mode. A non-dedicated file server, which isn't allowed in Versions 3.0 and higher, can be run in either console mode or operating system mode.

CSMA/CD   A method of data transmission within a network that avoids data collision by having each workstation check to see whether the cable is free before attempting to transmit. The abbreviation is for Carrier Sense Multiple Access with Collision Detection.

Dedicated File Server
A dedicated file server cannot be used as a workstation. This type of file server can only be operated in console mode. Under NetWare 386, all file servers must be run in dedicated mode.

Directory Attribute
A directory attribute is a special right that applies to a certain directory. Directory

attributes (also called directory masks) take precedence over rights granted to individual users.

Directory Structure

A directory structure defines how data is stored on a disk. Files are stored in directories and directories are stored in several levels. For example, one directory may contain several related subdirectories.

Diskless Workstations

This is a workstation that doesn't have its own boot diskette. Instead, it is booted directly from the file server. This type of workstation is not possible under NetWare Lite.

File Attribute

A file attribute or a file flag is used to define the ways in which the file may be accessed. File flags take precedence over other types of access rights.

File Locking

This is a mechanism that is used to prevent two or more users from writing to the same file on the network simultaneously. The first user to access a given file will effectively lock it, making it unavailable to other users. When the file lock is removed, another user can access the file as usual.

File Server

The file server is the master computer of the network. The network system and all its resources, including network drives, network printers, and utility and application programs, are managed from the file server.

Interleave

The Interleave indicates how many revolutions the hard disk has to make in order to read or write one complete track. The interleave factor is set when you format the hard disk. This determines the speed at which data can be stored and retrieved.

An interleave factor of 1 means that an entire track can be read in a single revolution of the disk. All consecutive sectors of the track are read in a single operation. With an interleave factor of two, only every other sector on the track is read, which means it takes two revolutions of the hard disk to read the track completely.

LAN

Local Area Network. A network that is located in a single building.

Logical Drive

A logical drive is a directory that has been assigned a drive letter. This directory is then accessed with the drive letter rather than the directory name. So you don't have to type in the name of a frequently used directory. Logical drive assignments are made with the Map command.

Login

Before you can use the network system, you must establish a software connection with the file server. This is done with the NetWare command Login. This command is also used to provide your username and a password (in most cases).

Logout

After you've ended your session on the network, you must disconnect from the file server in such a way that all the files you opened will be closed. Only after properly disconnecting from the file server can you safely switch off the power on your workstation. This is done with the NetWare command Logout.

Network Adapter

A network adapter is an expansion card that must be installed in every computer that you want to connect to your network. The network adapter and the cable are the hardware components of a workstation's network connection.

Node Address

A Node Address is a NetWare-specific address associated with a workstation. Every workstation has both a network address, which identifies the network, and its own node address.

A network address is similar to a postal zip code and the node address is similar to the address of a single house.

Non-Dedicated File Server

As opposed to a dedicated file server, a non-dedicated file server can be operated in either the console or the operating system mode. In Version 3.0 and higher (NetWare 386), file servers cannot be run in non-dedicated mode.

Password

In addition to a user name, a user is usually assigned a password that is also needed in order to log in to the system. Using passwords provides a higher level of security in your system, because it's more difficult for unauthorized individuals to gain access.

Print Job

Any output sent to a network printer is referred to as a print job. These jobs are sent to print queues, where they are processed in the order in which they are received.

Print Server

A print server is a computer that is dedicated to managing print queues and print jobs. Although a file server or any workstation can be set up as a print server, this computer will then be dedicated to printing and won't be able to perform any other tasks.

Queue

A queue is a list of jobs that are waiting to be processed. A job is a function, such as printing, storing or archiving data. Queues are given names so that any network program can access them. The jobs in a queue are processed in the order in which they are received.

Record Locking

Record locking, like file locking, is a form of data sharing in a network environment. However, instead of locking an entire file as with file locking, record locking only prevents access to individual records in a file while they're being used by another user.

Ring

A network topology in which the workstations are connected to one another in the form of a circle or ring.

Root Directory

The root directory is the highest level directory on a given disk or volume. Various subdirectories (such as SYSTEM, PUBLIC, LOGIN, etc.) can exist under the root directory.

Search Drive   A search drive (search path) is a directory, in which the operating system will search for files it needs but couldn't find in the current directory. NetWare uses the Map command to define search drives.

Semaphore   Semaphores are used to limit the number of workstations that can access a certain program simultaneously or to limit the number of programs a single network resource can use at once.

Shell   The shell is the software connection between a workstation and a file server. The operating system of the workstation is linked to the network operating system using the shell so that it can access all network resources. Under NetWare, the file that contains the shell is called IPX.COM. This file must be available on the boot diskette of each workstation and it must be executed before a user can log in to a file server.

Subdirectory   A subdirectory is a directory that is located below another directory in the directory structure of a disk. Subdirectories help you keep your files organized. A subdirectory can also contain additional subdirectories.

System Manager   The system manager (Supervisor) is responsible for keeping the system secure and working properly. The system manager creates and deletes user names, assigns passwords and access rights, etc. The following is a brief list of the system manager's major responsibilities:

- Create new user names.

- Delete user names.

- Assign access rights to individual users.

- Create special user menu systems.

- Install new application programs.

- Inform users of their responsibilities (e.g., deleting data that is no longer needed).

- Checking data security.

- Data backup.

- Monitor the load on the file server processor.

- Monitor the load on the processors of individual workstations.

- Manage the network disks.

- Delete programs that are no longer needed.

The system manager should be a responsible person who is very familiar with the operations of the network.

Task

A task is a single action initiated by a user. A read operation on a file, copying a file, and deleting a file are all examples of tasks.

Token Passing

A method of data transmission on a network in which a token is passed from one workstation to another. Only the workstation that "owns" the token can transmit data.

Topology

Describes the physical connections of a network; examples are: bus, ring and star.

User Name

A user name is required before you can log in to the network system. The system manager (SUPERVISOR) assigns user names to all users. In addition to a user name, each user is normally assigned a password. The user name and password must be supplied each time a user logs in.

WAN

Wide Area Network. A network in which the workstations or resources are located in different buildings.

Workstation

A workstation refers to a computer that is physically connected to the network and can access network resources.

Appendix D: Error And Status Messages

This appendix contains a list of the status reports displayed by NetWare Lite. A brief explanation of the cause of the error and suggestions on how to correct it are also included, when necessary.

> **Status Report 1: NetWare Lite - Version 1.1 Copyright (c)1991, Novell, Inc., All Rights Reserved.**

This message is given when SERVER.EXE is loaded. It displays the version number of SERVER.EXE.

No action is necessary.

> **Status Report 2: SERVER.EXE was already in memory; it was not loaded again.**

This message informs you that a second attempt was made to load SERVER.EXE.

It is possible that a call to SERVER.EXE exists in two separate startup files on the system, for example the AUTOEXEC.BAT and STARTNET.BAT files.

Although the problem should be corrected, it will have no effect on the operation of the network.

> **Status Report 3: SERVER.EXE was loaded successfully.**

This message informs you that SERVER.EXE was successfully loaded.

No action is neccessary.

> **Status Report 4: SERVER.EXE was not loaded because DOS 3.0 (or above) was not in memory.**

DOS 3.0 or above is required to use this version of SERVER.EXE.

In order to use SERVER.EXE you will have to upgrade to a version of DOS later than 3.0.

> **Status Report 5: DOS SHARE was not executed before an attempt to load SERVER.EXE; SERVER.EXE will be loaded anyway.**

The DOS program SHARE enables file sharing in a network or multitasking environment. SHARE must be loaded prior to working with NetWare Lite.

Although the SERVER.EXE program will be loaded, there is now the possibility of data collision on the network. You should reboot the file server, and make sure SHARE is loaded before SERVER.EXE. To load SHARE, either insert the following line, before the call to SERVER.EXE, in the start up file (usually STARTNET.BAT):

```
SHARE
```

or enter the following command at the DOS prompt, before loading SERVER.EXE:

```
SHARE  Enter
```

> **Status Report 6: SERVER.EXE was not loaded because IPXODI.COM had not been executed.**

IPXODI.COM enables the workstation to communicate with the file server. It must be loaded before SERVER.EXE.

You must make sure that IPXODI.COM is loaded before SERVER.EXE. Please see Chapter 3 for information on loading IPXODI and the STARTNET.BAT file.

> **Status Report 7: SERVER.EXE was not loaded because the NetWare Lite configuration file could not be found.**

The INSTALL program will save the configuration options of the network card in a file named NET.CFG. This message is given if SERVER.EXE cannot find or access this file.

You should rerun the INSTALL program to set up the NET.CFG file before continuing work with NetWare Lite.

> **Status Report 8: NetWare Lite CLIENT.EXE - Version 1.0 Copyright (c) 1991, Novell, Inc. All Rights Reserved.**

This message is given when CLIENT.EXE is loaded. It displays the version number of CLIENT.EXE.

No action is necessary.

> **Status Report 9: SERVER.EXE was not loadable because its version and the version of NET.EXE are incompatible.**

The version numbers of the different NetWare Lite program files are stored and compared. This message will be given when the current version of SERVER.EXE is not compatible with the other NetWare Lite files.

One possible way to correct the error is to reinstall NetWare Lite on the computer.

> **Status Report 10: SERVER.EXE will be loaded even though the FILES= parameter in CONFIG.SYS is lower than 30, the minimum suggested.**

The following line, found in the CONFIG.SYS file, limits the number of files that can be opened at any given time.

```
FILES=xx
```

Novell recommends this number be set to 30. You should edit this line in the CONFIG.SYS file so that it appears as:

```
FILES=30
```

> **Status Report 11: The printer area control file for a defined printer was not found. SERVER.EXE created one with the default values.**

SERVER.EXE could not find the control file used for one of the network printers.

If a control file is not found, SERVER.EXE will create one using the default values. If changes must be made, use the NET utility to modify the printer settings.

> **Status Report 12: CLIENT.EXE was loaded successfully.**

This message informs you that CLIENT.EXE was successfully loaded.

No action is neccessary.

> **Status Report 13: CLIENT.EXE is already in memory; it was not loaded again.**

This message informs you that a second attempt was made to load CLIENT.EXE.

It's possible that a call to CLIENT.EXE exists in two separate startup files on the system, for example the AUTOEXEC.BAT and STARTNET.BAT files.

Although the problem should be corrected, it will have no effect on the operation of the network.

> **Status Report 14: CLIENT.EXE is not loaded because DOS 3.0 (or above) was not in memory.**

DOS 3.0 or above is required to use this version of CLIENT.EXE.

In order to use CLIENT.EXE you will have to upgrade to a version of DOS later than 3.0.

> **Status Report 15: CLIENT.EXE was not loaded because IPXODI.COM had not been executed.**

IPXODI.COM enables the workstation to communicate with the file server. It must be loaded before SERVER.EXE.

You must make sure that IPXODI.COM is loaded before SERVER.EXE. Please see Chapter 3 for information on loading IPXODI and the STARTNET.BAT file.

> **Status Report 16: Novell IPX Protocol Vx.x (date) (C) copyright 1990 Novell, Inc. All Rights Reserved.**

This message is given when IPXODI.COM is loaded. It displays the version number of IPXODI.COM currently being used.

> **Status Report 17: Print jobs were found in printer area. All jobs were placed on HOLD.**

When the file server last went down, there were print jobs waiting to be printed. All jobs waiting to be printed will be saved when the server goes down and placed on hold.

You can use the NET utility to delete or print the jobs that were placed on hold.

Status Report 18: FATAL: IPX already loaded.

An attempt was made to load IPXODI after IPXODI or IPX had been loaded. This file is used for communication on the network and should only be loaded once.

It's possible that a call to IPXODI.COM exists in two separate startup files on the system, for example the AUTOEXEC.BAT and STARTNET.BAT files.

Although the problem should be corrected, it will have no effect on the operation of the network.

Status Report 19: The printer area control file for a defined printer was not found. SERVER.EXE created one with default values.

SERVER.EXE could not find the control file used for one of the network printers.

If a control file is not found, SERVER.EXE will create one using the default values. If changes must be made, use the NET utility to modify the printer settings.

Status Report 20: Novell Link Support Layer Vx.x (data) (C) Copyright 1990 Novell, Inc. All Rights Reserved.

This message is given when LSL.COM is loaded. It displays the version number of LSL.COM currently being used.

Status Report 21: The user database file is corrupt or missing.

SERVER.EXE uses a special file to control the network users. This message indicates that SERVER.EXE could not find or access this file.

If there is more than one server on the network, it may be possible to use NET LOGIN to log in from one of the other servers. This should update the user database file on all servers.

If the problem occurs on the only server, or the NET LOGIN procedure does not work, you will have to reinstall NetWare Lite.

Status Report 22: FATAL: LSL already loaded.

An attempt was made to load IPXODI after IPXODI or IPX had been loaded. This file is used for communication on the network and should only be loaded once.

It's possible that a call to IPXODI.COM exists in two separate startup files on the system, for example the AUTOEXEC.BAT and STARTNET.BAT files.

Although the problem should be corrected, it will have no effect on the operation of the network.

Status Report 23: CLIENT.EXE was not loaded because an IPX Socket could not be opened. Please configure IPX with more sockets before loading CLIENT.EXE.

The settings used by IPXODI.COM or IPX.COM must be modified.

Please see the documentation that accompanied your version of IPXODI.COM or IPX.COM for further information on how to change these settings.

Status Report 24: SERVER.EXE cannot initialize network printer.

SERVER.EXE could not initialize one of the network printers.

You should check to see whether the printer is connected and functioning properly.

You may also use the NET utility to delete and re-install the network printer. This will update all control files, and should correct the problem.

Status Report 25: More network directories and printers have been defined than are allowed by the configuration of SERVER.EXE.

The network manager can limit the number of network directories and printers using the NET utility. This message is displayed when the number of network printers and directories exceeds the set limit.

The items that were created after the limit was reached will not be loaded. You should either increase the limits or remove any network printers or directories that are no longer being used.

Status Report 26: The file that defines network directories and printers is corrupt or missing.

The file used to keep track of the network printers and directories could not be found.

If only certain directories or printers are effected, you can delete and re-install these instead of reinstalling NetWare Lite.

If all network printers and directories are affected, it may be neccessary to re-install NetWare Lite.

Status Report 27: SERVER.EXE was loaded but is not operational.

This message will be displayed if there was a problem loading SERVER.EXE. It will be accompanied by another message which describes the problem in detail.

Status Report 28: SERVER.EXE could not update printer control information. The printer may need to be re-started for printer attributes to take effect.

If SERVER.EXE is unable to update the network printer information, this message will be displayed.

Re-load SERVER.EXE and this will often correct the problem. If the problem persists, delete and re-create the network printer.

Status Report 29: The user database file is corrupt or missing.

SERVER.EXE uses a special file to control the network users. This message indicates that SERVER.EXE could not find or access this file.

If there is more than one server on the network, it may be possible to use NET LOGIN to log in from one of the other servers. This should update the user database file on all servers.

If the problem occurs on the only server, or the NET LOGIN procedure does not work, you will have to re-install NetWare Lite.

Status Report 30: Error opening IPX Socket.

The settings used by IPXODI.COM or IPX.COM must be modified.

Please see the documentation that accompanied your version of
IPXODI.COM or IPX.COM for additional information on how to
change these settings.

**Status Report 31: Print jobs were found in the printer area. All
jobs were placed on HOLD.**

When the file server last went down, there were print jobs waiting
to be printed. All jobs waiting to be printed will be saved when the
server goes down and placed on hold.

You can use the NET utility to delete or print the jobs that were
placed on hold.

**Status Report 32: The size of receive buffers specified in the
server configuration is too big for the LAN card being used. The
receive buffer size was changed to the maximum packet size
allowed by the LAN card.**

An invalid entry was made when configuring the server. NetWare
Lite corrected this entry.

No action is necessary.

**Status Report 33: The size of read buffers specified in the server
configuration is too big for the LAN card being used. The read
buffer size was changed to the maximum packet size allowed
by the LAN card.**

An invalid entry was made when configuring the server. NetWare
Lite corrected this entry.

No action is necessary.

**Status Report 34: SERVER.EXE cannot initialize network
printer because the number of configured printers is too small.**

The server configuration would not allow one (or more) of the
network printers to be loaded.

You should use the NET utility program to adjust the number of
network printers allowed, as described in Chapter 9.

> **Status Report 35: SERVER.EXE cannot initialize network printer because the number of configured printers is too small.**

The server configuration would not allow one (or more) of the network printers to be loaded.

You should use the NET utility program to adjust the number of network printers allowed, as described in Chapter 9.

> **Status Report 36: Selected configuration of SERVER.EXE exceeds 64K of data memory. Use NET.EXE to reduce configuration parameters. Reboot computer now, then reconfigure server with NET.EXE while SERVER.EXE is not loaded.**

With the current configuration of the server, SERVER.EXE exceeds the amount of memory allowed.

You should use the NET utility to adjust the number of connections and size of the buffers to reduce the amount of memory required by SERVER .EXE.

> **Status Report 37: CLIENT.EXE was loaded before SERVER.EXE. SERVER.EXE should be loaded first if a Network Printer is, or will be, attached to this computer.**

If network printers are attached to the computer, SERVER.EXE must be loaded before CLIENT.EXE.

You should unload SERVER.EXE and CLIENT.EXE and load in the proper sequence. If the network drivers are loaded from a batch file (e.g., STARTNET.BAT, AUTOEXEC.BAT) this change should be made in the batch file.

> **Status Report 38: Not enough memory to load.**

Not enough memory.

> **Status Report 39: The IO buffer size specified in the server configuration is not a multiple of 16. The IO buffer size was changed to a multiple of 16.**

An invalid entry was made when configuring the server. NetWare Lite corrected this entry.

You should use the NET utility to make the change acceptable.

> **Status Report 40: The IO buffer size multiplier specified by the server configuration is not a valid multiple of the receive buffer size. The IO buffer size was changed to 2 times the receive buffer size.**

An invalid entry was made when configuring the server. NetWare Lite corrected this entry.

You should use the NET utility to make the change acceptable.

> **Status Report 41: The number of IO buffers specified in the server configuration is greater than the number of connections. The number of cache buffers was changed to the number of connections.**

An invalid entry was made when configuring the server. NetWare Lite corrected this entry.

You should use the NET utility to make the change acceptable.

> **Status Report 42: Byte value greater than 255 in configuration file was truncated.**

An illegal entry in the configuration file was corrected by NetWare Lite.

No action is necessary.

> **Status Report 43: CLIENT.EXE was not unloaded because it is not currently loaded.**

Although CLIENT.EXE was not loaded, an attempt was made to unload it from memory.

No action is necessary.

> **Status Report 44: CLIENT.EXE was not unloaded because the version of CLIENT.EXE in memory is not the same as this one. You must run the same version of CLIENT.EXE in order to unload it.**

Two different versions of CLIENT.EXE exist on the computer. The version called to unload CLIENT.EXE is not the same as the one originally loaded.

You should determine which version of CLIENT.EXE is current and remove the other copy from the system.

Status Report 45: CLIENT.EXE was not unloaded because another program was loaded after it. You must unload this other program first in order to unload CLIENT.EXE.

All programs loaded after CLIENT.EXE must be unloaded before CLIENT.EXE can be unloaded.

Status Report 46: CLIENT.EXE was unloaded from memory.

This message is displayed to inform you that CLIENT.EXE has been succesfully removed from memory.

No action is necessary.

Status Report 47: Byte value greater than 255 in NET.CFG configuration file was truncated.

An illegal entry in the NET.CFG file was corrected by NetWare Lite.

No action is necessary.

Status Report 48: Bad route address syntax in NET.CFG configuration file.

The NET.CFG file is incorrect or damaged.

Status Report 49: SERVER.EXE was not unloaded because it is not currently loaded.

Although SERVER.EXE was not loaded, an attempt was made to unload it from memory.

No action is necessary.

Status Report 50: SERVER.EXE was not unloaded because the version of SERVER.EXE in memory is not the same as this one. You must run the same version of SERVER.EXE in order to unload it.

Two different versions of SERVER.EXE exist on the computer. The version called to unload SERVER.EXE is not the same as the one originally loaded.

You should determine which version of SERVER.EXE is current and remove the other copy from the system.

> **Status Report 51: SERVER.EXE was not unloaded because another program was loaded after it. You must unload this other program first in order to unload SERVER.EXE.**

All programs loaded after SERVER.EXE must be unloaded before SERVER.EXE can be unloaded.

> **Status Report 52: SERVER.EXE was unloaded from memory.**

This message is displayed to inform you that SERVER.EXE has been successfully removed from memory.

No action is necessary.

> **Status Report 53: This copy of SERVER.EXE is for update use only. SERVER.EXE did not load.**

This version of SERVER.EXE is from an update diskette, not a Netware Lite diskette.

> **Status Report 54: This copy of CLIENT.EXE is for update use only. CLIENT.EXE did not load.**

This version of CLIENT.EXE is from an update diskette, not a Netware Lite diskette.

> **Report 55: SERVER.EXE was not loaded because an IPX socket could not be opened. Please configure IPX with more sockets before loading SERVER.EXE.**

The settings used by IPXODI.COM or IPX.COM must be modified.

Please see the documentation that accompanied your version of IPXODI.COM or IPX.COM for additional information on how to change these settings.

> **Status Report 56: SERVER.EXE was not loaded because NETx.COM has been loaded. Please load SERVER.EXE before loading NETx.COM.**

You must load SERVER.EXE before loading NETx.COM (used with native NetWare).

If you are loading the network drivers from a batch file (e.g., STARTNET.BAT, AUTOEXEC.BAT) you should change the order in which the drivers are called.

Index

V-Z

Abacus
pc catalog
Order Toll Free 1-800-451-4319

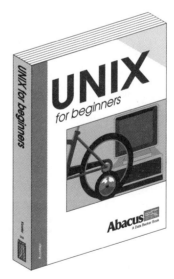

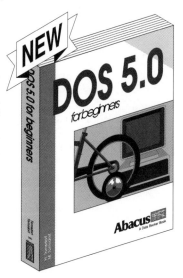